My
Spirit
Moose

My Spirit Moose

The Place of the Hunter in the Nature of Things

Ralph Gibbins

To order additional copies of this book, contact:
Xlibris Corporation
1-888-795-4274
www.Xlibris.com
Orders@Xlibris.com
45804

CONTENTS

ACKNOWLEDGEMENTS

Many friends, acquaintances, and some perfect strangers helped me in the preparation of this book, and I extend my special thanks to the following people.

My wife, Joan, who gave unbelievable encouragement, helped gather material, and became my official and tireless sounding board.

Author and retired publishing executive Peter Taylor who patiently offered editorial advice and helped me hone my writing skills.

Publishing guru Jim Chalmers and his wife Karen who gave advise and encouragement along the way.

My brother Ron's support in supplying photos and reference materials is much appreciated.

Eli Thib, and Ken Bryan, both deceased now, who shared their knowledge generously.

Retired police officer Frank MacEachern and wife Judy who offered advise and photos.

Brian Henry who offered valuable guidance in his workshops for writers.

Roger Irwin for permission to use his moose photo on the front cover.

Anyone I have not included in this list, I look forward to thanking in person.

I accept full responsibility for any errors or omissions.

Finally, of course, I am extremely grateful for all my experiences.

Ralph Gibbins
Toronto, Ontario 2007

FOREWORD

What to Say to a Person Who Has Never Hunted
Foreword By Dr. Randall L. Eaton,
An Internationally Recognized Authority on Animal
Behaviour, Wildlife Conservation and Human Evolution

Who is the greatest conservationist in the history of the world? The answer is, "The best known hunter in the history of the world," Teddy Roosevelt. What few people know is that he was the first man to write about women's rights, the subject of his senior thesis at Harvard. The paradox perplexes ecofeminists. Does hunting teach violence? What do you think Jimmy Carter and Nelson Mandela would say? They both received the Nobel Peace prize—and both are avid hunters.

In a questionnaire survey I did of 2500 hunters, average age of 55, 97% male, I asked what events in their lives opened their hearts and engendered compassion in them. The prevailing choice by women was "becoming a parent," but for men it was "taking the life of an animal."

The polarities of human life consist of women bringing life into the world and men taking life to support life. For hundreds of thousands of years boys had to kill an animal of sufficient size to prove they could provide and thus qualify for manhood and marriage.

Hunting is still the most profound rite of passage from boyhood to manhood.

The same survey revealed that 82% of recreational hunters thank the animals they kill or the Creator. The words they chose to express how they feel about the animals they hunt were, "respect," "admiration" and "reverence." Not unlike Native American hunters. Michael Gurian, author of the best-selling The Wonder of Boys, says in my TV production, "Respect and Responsibility: The Truth About Kids Who Hunt," that, "Hunting teaches compassion."

In the same production, Dr. Don Trent Jacobs, revolutionary educator and author of Teaching Virtues Across the Curriculum, states, "Hunting is the ideal way to teach young people universal virtues including patience, generosity, courage, fortitude and humility." He defines humility as knowing you are part of something greater than yourself. At one time, Jacobs directed the largest wilderness centre in the world for juvenile delinquents.

The most successful program ever conducted for juvenile delinquents was at the School for Urban and Wilderness Studies in southern Idaho. For 13 years groups of boys went into the wilderness with nothing but a sleeping bag and a pocketknife. Their only food was what they could gather or catch and kill. According to follow-up surveys conducted one year after they left, 85% of the boys had not got into trouble during that year. Dr. Wade Brackenbury, who led the boys, is convinced that it was taking the lives of small animals for food that had the greatest influence on the boys' transformation.

Dr. Helen Smith of Knoxville wrote Scarred Hearts. She is a leading authority on violent kids (who kill). In an interview in "Respect and Responsibility," she said, "Columbine never would have happened if those boys had been properly mentored in hunting and shooting."

In the same production, Dr. Jim Rose, adolescent neuropsychologist at the University of Wyoming says, "Hunting teaches self-control and respect for life," and, "Learning to use a firearm teaches responsibility." Dr. Scott Cutting, a psychologist in South Carolina, successfully used shooting to heal young men of serious aggression.

A few years ago, the BATF and FBI conducted a study and could not find a single instance of a young person committing a felony with a legally owned firearm, which indicates that kids mentored in hunting and shooting use firearms for the right reasons.

Gurian, Jacobs, Smith and Rose all highly recommend and endorse hunting and shooting for youth.

Which of the following well known Americans were hunters?

Thomas Jefferson
John James Audubon
David Thoreau
Teddy Roosevelt

George Eastman
John Steinbeck
Aldo Leopold
Clark Gable
Ernest Hemmingway
Jimmy Stewart
Jimmy Carter

That's right, all of the above.

Did you know that hunters were the original environmental conservationists and they still lead in that field? Did you know that 700,000 members of Ducks Unlimited have successfully conserved over 12 million acres of wildlife habitat to the benefit of the entire living community of North America? That the Rocky Mountain Elk Foundation has conserved over four million acres and reintroduced elk throughout its former range in the midwest and eastern U.S.? That there may be more wild turkeys and deer in the U.S. than at any time in history?

When the rest of the environmental community is waging rear-guard actions, the hunting community is on the offensive. The truth is that hunting is a model for sustainability. For those who participate directly in it the food chain becomes a love chain. Hunters put their money where their hearts are.

INTRODUCTION

This book about discovering qualities in nature was prompted by my encounter while on a hunting trip with an exceptionally large bull moose and an ensuing conversation with an associate of my wife who offered insights to her about the moose and the meaning of my experience with him. She called him a *spirit moose*. Her thoughts intrigued me, so when she came to visit my wife, I took the opportunity to question her on the source of her information. She mentioned several books on native beliefs about animals and their relationship with man. She also mentioned that she was not sure of the source of all of her thoughts, which is true for most of us if we wonder about such things at all.

Anyone interested in conserving wildlife, about ethics in hunting, reducing crime and increasing security, improving health and happiness will find ideas in this book that should be helpful.

CHAPTER 1

The encounter

The world around us bears signs of both order and chaos.
—Richard Tarnas (scientist, educator, and author)

Nature and Nature's laws lay hid in night:
God said, Let Newton be! And all was light.

—Alexander Pope

My spirit moose experience is a true story. The incident happened in the fall of the new millennium. The encounter started me down a path of investigation that helped clarify my feelings about hunting, and this in turn stirred me to try my hand at writing.

Our hunting ground was a rugged wilderness area. The only other hunters nearby were bears and wolves.

We had been struggling for several days, hoping to get a peek at the moose we knew were close by because of all the signs—hoof tracks, beds, rut pits, and fresh dung. We even heard them as they skilfully stayed just out of sight.

The flu bug hit the camp, and one afternoon while the hunters were taking a nap, my seventy-five-year-old ailing cousin announced as he crawled out of his sleeping bag, "We are not going to find a moose here. I am going over the portage to the far bay to try calling." ("Calling" is an attempt to imitate the sound of a moose looking for a mate, thus luring one.)

I went with him, but we had no luck. On our way back, on an impulse, we stopped and wandered down a trail to a little lake.

It was a beautiful evening. The lake, like a mirror, reflected colour from the sky and trees. Although the main rut (mating season) was over, I gave my cow call using a birch bark horn then sat on a log and waited. There was a brooding silence—could I only know the secret of the subtle charm that fills these lonely places. I mused over our successes and failures over sixty years of hunting and how hard we worked to occasionally get lucky. I observed a lonely loon and wondered why he had not gone south—maybe he was a weak link and would perish at nature's hands.

Three small otters appeared and gradually gravitated towards me as they playfully dove and swam quietly in the water. Occasionally, they stopped to curiously peer at me while sitting erect with front paws in a begging fashion, not moving a hair so they looked like stumps in the water. I wondered what spirit took me to this magical moment.

The setting where the encounter occurred.

Suddenly, I was jolted from my reverie by a thunderous crack from my cousin's rifle. My head turned quickly towards him as he shouldered his gun and fired again. I crawled across the rocks to him and whispered, "What in hell are you shooting at?"

"There is a huge bull moose standing on the far shore. I think I hit him. He is like a ghost. Look for the white whiskers on his legs. My gun is jamming," he whispered.

I caught sight of the white whiskers; and immediately, a large moose came into focus, standing and looking at us. *I'll be damned*, I thought. *He liked my cow call.*

It was a long shot. I rested my .30-06 on my knee, aimed, and fired. He turned slowly and started up the steep bank. I could see his entire back and fired again. He seemed to stumble as he veered left and turned back along the shoreline. We fired several more shots before the moose disappeared. Did we hit him? It was too late in the day to find out, so I took a compass bearing for direction next day.

In the camp that night, there were ten experts with lots of questions. How far away was he? Which guns and what shells had we used? How many inches high did we aim? Frank, one of the more experienced members of our group, said, "I know you are both good shots. It would have to be a charmed moose to dodge all those bullets."

Next morning, we portaged a canoe and paddled to the target area where we found his tracks on the shore and a spot of blood on the grass. We lost his tracks where he headed into the dense underbrush and over hard rocky ground, but by crisscrossing around the area, we found more blood spots on the fallen leaves—or were they just the normal red in the fall leaves? Sometimes, it was hard to tell. Then, there were obvious red pools of blood that began to appear more frequently. We were able to follow these markings and, with each step, gained confidence that we would soon find our moose. We noticed where he had rested several times, and this led us to believe that he had been seriously wounded; otherwise, he would have run non-stop for many miles.

After three hours of tracking, the blood spots mysteriously disappeared. Our faces dropped. How could this be? After further analysis, we concluded that he was wounded in his front left leg and that if we did not disturb him he would not travel far. We believed that in his weakened state, he would lie down to rest, lose more blood, become weaker, and perhaps perish. Therefore, we concluded it would be best to leave and return the next day to continue our search. To find our way back to the exact location in the dense bush, we blazed a trail using orange marker tape.

"This tape is a great invention," I commented for the benefit and amusement of the young folk. "Easier than blazing with an axe and much better than toilet paper."

Next morning, we returned with more help and a plan for cornering our prey. My task was to ribbon a trail east to a sheer rock cliff that no moose could climb. Others in the party were to take positions along this trail where they could watch for our quarry. Two others were to travel in a semicircle, first heading south into the wind and then arcing west and north. Considering the wind and terrain, we reckoned this strategy gave us the best chance of finding our moose and, if he was alive, he would run north towards the waiting hunters. We realized that lacking the hunting talents of a wolf, our efforts were like looking for a needle in a haystack. Nonetheless, we hoped lady luck, combined with our limited human skills, would bring success.

I snapped the cover over the front lens of the scope on my rifle to keep it clean of pine needles and other dirt then started heading east, pushing my way through the dense bush.

About an hour later, as I scrambled up towards the rock wall, I heard a shout from the south, "We have found blood!"

I took a compass bearing and, alive with excitement, started moving slowly and quietly towards the voice through thick balsams that severely limited my vision. Suddenly, a monstrous bull jumped up just feet in front of me! His rack was huge, and his eyes met mine! I threw my gun to my shoulder while releasing the safety. Damn it, I had forgotten the scope cover. Quickly, I snapped it off, but it was too late—the animal vanished down a steep cliff. For a few seconds, he sounded like an express train crashing through the bush, then came dead silence.

"He came close to me!" Ken shouted. "I could see branches moving but not him."

We found pools of blood and congregated to marshal our forces. Three of our group had to leave to return to the city, so the plan was that I would take them back to camp and get more help. The others were to wait until I fired a signal shot on my return, wait a half hour to give me time to position the new people, and then, they would resume tracking. We were confident that we would corner our prey.

On my return two hours later, I signalled and headed into the bush with my recruits. A half hour later, we found fresh blood spots. I congratulated myself on my animal and bush savvy but soon began to wonder why the moose had arrived ahead of us.

Could it be that my friends had not waited for my signal? Yes. In their impatience, they had started tracking and caused the moose to move from his resting place. They further compounded their error by continued tracking. They were sure he was about to drop.

We asked ourselves, What kind of charmed life did this moose live and what kind of endurance possessed him?

We started to follow the spots of blood again. But they disappeared.

That night, I related how surprised I was when this great animal jumped up so close to me and how he would normally have met his maker with one quick shot. I commented on his unusually shaped large antlers. I felt sad and frustrated. Why had I forgotten the scope cover? The moose was so close to me that at that range, I should have pulled the trigger anyway. How could such a large wounded animal move so quickly? Why had experienced hunters disregarded our agreed-upon plan? I kept seeing this enormous moose jumping up in front of me with his huge eyes and antlers directed down at me! Why had he not charged? He could have flattened me easily.

The next day, we commenced our search again. Nothing went right. My buddies lost their way. I was led in circles several times by tracks and blood spots that crisscrossed; then late in the day, the signs disappeared again. The next day, heavy rain shut us down; and the following day, we had to leave for Toronto.

*   *   *

Back in Toronto, I kept thinking about that moose every day. I felt a calling to make another trip north at the first snowfall, which would make tracking much easier. I tried to rationalize my unusually deep feelings. Leaving a wounded animal was distasteful. Also, bagging a prize animal probably appealed to my ego. However, getting frozen in was a definite concern at that time of year.

CHAPTER 2

A mysterious message and ensuing information

The unnatural, that too is natural.

—Goethe

My wife's associate mentioned earlier is considered by many to have psychic abilities. My wife had mentioned to her in a telephone conversation that I had been hunting, that I had wounded a moose, and that I was considering another trip north to try to find it.

The psychic lady had interrupted to say, "That was a very special moose!"

She referred to it as a spirit moose, explaining that in all animal species, one occasionally appears whose purpose is to strengthen the breed. She said that his work was not yet finished; therefore, his wound would heal, and I was not to be concerned. She pointed out that a seriously wounded animal would normally stand and fight or charge his adversary. She claimed that neither I, nor anyone else, would ever see him again; and the reason the moose jumped up at me was so I would see what a special animal he was. She also said that he wanted me to know he understood me and intended to raise my awareness to a new level.

My interest was tweaked by her comments, so I had a further discussion with her in which she offered additional thoughts. She explained that the spirit moose wanted me to focus on guiding other people to a higher awareness about hunting because many people do not fully appreciate the significance of a system where all life depends on one species feeding on another and where controlling overpopulation and weeding out the weak by hunting is consistent with nature's way, the survival of the fittest, and the fostering of healthy stock. Animals grow stronger and wiser in their attempts to avoid being caught. The strongest, most alert, and most knowledgeable survive. It is unfortunate that many people relate hunting to the slaughter of the buffalo rather than actual causes, which were all the activities associated with the greed of Western civilization for skins and hats as well as the army and settlers who were taking over the land for cattle, sheep, crops, and supporting services. Hunting is a natural and necessary component of nature when done in an appropriate way and is as old as life itself. The misunderstandings many people have, we agreed, are for the most part a result of an urban lifestyle that isolates people from the realities of the natural world.

The psychic also said that a patch on my wife's leg would heal like the moose's wound. The next day, the doctor informed my wife that a biopsy showed that there was no malignancy. The patch had healed. A bit of a coincidence, I speculated.

I am sceptical of psychics. However, this person is very genuine, and many people claim they have gained insights through her. I am also prepared to consider that there are many mysteries in life that are beyond my comprehension. According to Indian folklore, animals can pass on wisdom to those who listen. Maybe there are more things in heaven and earth than science can account for. In any case, what happened was an interesting series of events.

Whatever else it was, the encounter was a catalyst that triggered further investigation, extensive reading, and numerous discussions about man's place in the natural world. Once it became known that I was proposing to write a book, the floodgates opened; and more people ventured opinions, stories, and even questions that led to further research. Over the following months, one observation that kept emerging throughout my explorations was the disconnection with nature and the natural world brought about by urbanization and, with that, the loss or disappearance of the many lessons that are part of the rural and wilderness experience. With more than 75 percent of our population living in cities today, the opportunity to learn from Mother Nature, to learn what the seasons provide, and to learn where food comes from have almost disappeared. Like the many who have spoken and written about our drift from nature and the perspectives provided by the natural world, I can only hope my observations will offer readers much food for thought. Even in the daily clash and chaos of our urban landscape, a voice in the wilderness has much to say if we are willing to listen.

If you talk to the animals they will talk with you and you will
know each other.
If you do not talk to them you will not know them, and what you
do not know you will fear.
What one fears one destroys.

—Chief Dan George

Hunting has become an extremely contentious issue in our modern world. People for their own reasons, and often armed with little in the way of solid evidence, have chosen sides—each side shouting the other down, disinclined to hear the other out. Personally, and for many years, I struggled with my own conscience and feelings about the sport. The pros and cons, as I considered each, made one thing clear: a full understanding of any complex issue can never be settled effectively by the loudest voice, a single argument, or by a one-sided approach. In any attempt to reach a consensus, one must examine the pros and cons, the "good" and the "bad," as carefully as possible. It is then, and only then, in my experience that a person avoids the confusion and false beliefs that "jumping to conclusions" brings to debate of any kind. This book is an attempt to do just that—to hear both sides, to examine the information, and to relive the experiences that brought me to a pro-hunting side.

As with many such public debates, there are aspects of hunting that are not easily understood. And as is also true about such debate, the missing ingredient is all too often the sharing of experiences and solid information between protagonists.

What I hope to do in this book is present information that will help reframe notions about hunting and nature, ideas that I feel will be helpful to society in general and which may serve as a bridge between hunters on the one hand and the large general public of intelligent readers on the other hand—those readers who have never encountered sufficient grounds for accepting the possibility that hunting has any validity. Perhaps hunting itself, to be true to the task, must undergo a transformation of its own.

David Cumes, MD, in his book *Inner Passages, Outer Journeys: Wilderness, Healing, and the Discovery of Self* points out that there are modern-day hunters who appear fixated on a trophy but are mindful and meditative in their hunting experiences. He suggests we begin with a purpose, for example, to capture our prey; but once the intention is set, we need to disengage our craving for an explicit outcome. He cautions that when we focus on only one outcome, we lose the magic and the ability to heal and restore ourselves. He suggests that excessive goal orientation and rapture are mutually exclusive and claims we need to balance opposites to achieve "wilderness rapture." In this case, the opposites to which he refers are the two sides of a coin: one side stressing a need for goals and objectives, the other side claiming that enjoyment of participation in the process is the answer. This, we are told, is where the real gold is to be found. Such dilemmas are often called the dualities in life, or paradoxes. These are recurring pieces of the puzzles presented in this document.

The need for balancing, or reconciling opposites, was crucial to my arriving at a pro-hunting position; and I suggest a very important consideration for all of us relative to hunting and, in fact, for most activities in which we engage.

*   *   *

A survey by Environment Canada in 1996, *The Importance of Nature to Canadians*, states that approximately 11 percent of Canadians showed great or some interest in hunting but that only 5.1 percent hunt. My perspectives will be especially meaningful to these people. In addition, I have had conversations with many others who became interested when hunting was properly presented. This prompts me to think that the material in this book should be interesting to a broad range of readers, not just Canadians. Because of the global world in which we live, much of what I address has implications for people in other countries as well.

While I am not asking that you accept everything I say in this document, I do ask that you keep an open mind and heart to what I am trying to explain but for which words are often inadequate. At times, I may appear a tad critical. Nevertheless, my purpose is to inform and provide food for thought.

*   *   *

Man is an important factor in the management of natural elements in a world that is constantly changing. Man is also a part of nature, a creation that requires living matter for food. If we closely observe man's nature, I think we can agree that man tends to be, and needs to be, a perennial student—a student who, throughout the ages, learns much about himself and the universe through wilderness and hunting experiences.

All men by nature desire to know.

—Aristotle

The management of anything requires sound judgement and caution. For wildlife species, management implies treating them in a way that shows consideration for both the game hunted and the people who value them. Management can help maintain healthy populations of animals just for the sake of having those healthy populations, in addition to other reasons such as hunting. In this process, management creates and maintains habitat that supports many species while, at the same time, provides facilities for various healthy recreational pursuits and economic benefits for all of society.

Let me begin by summarizing some pertinent data. In Ontario, for example, over one hundred regions have been created called Wildlife Management Units. In each WMU, wildlife is monitored, and counts are made of the larger species. The number of animals that hunters can harvest is managed by hunting seasons and by a host of other regulations that vary by WMU and species. The number harvested ranges from zero to about 20 percent of the population, depending on region and animal. Record keeping has improved dramatically over the past century and especially in the past few years due in large part to hunting interests who want to sustain the resource for their recreation.

The overall population of wild animals has increased in North America over the last half century. A major factor in the increase are those hunting interests that have influenced the development of hunting regulations, protection of existing and provision of new habitat, and reintroduction of species such as wild turkey, Canada geese, and elk. Hunters have spent millions of dollars in efforts to sustain wildlife. One outstanding example is the millions of acres of habitat developed by Ducks Unlimited. In addition to ducks, thousands of other species benefit, including man who often visits the areas for outdoor recreation—the enjoyment of bird-watching and photography as well as hunting.

Dave Taylor—author, naturalist, and photographer—has done an extensive research on black bears across North America. In his book *Black Bears: A Natural History*, he reports that since the recognition of the black bear as a game animal and introduction of bear-hunting regulations in the early 1960s, "The increase in the continent's number of black bears has been phenomenal." He supports his assessment with data and says, "There could be as many as one million black bears alive in North America today

(2006)!"—an increase of about 300 percent compared with the population of three hundred thousand to four hundred thousand in 1966.

MORE DATA (Latest figures 2003)

	Total Population (Ontario)	Harvested by Licensed Hunters		Hunting Contribution to Gross Provincial Income
		North America	Ontario	
Black Bear	100,000	3%	5%	$32 Million
Moose	114,000	Unknown	7%	$93 Million
Deer	over 400,000	Unknown	20%	$91 Million
Total from Big Game				$216 Million
				(Taxes: $16 Million)
Wild Turkey				$9 Million

Volunteer hunters and the Ontario Federation of Anglers and Hunters (OFAH) in cooperation with Ministry of Natural Resources (MNR) imported from the United States and introduced 273 wild turkeys in late 1970.

Canada geese were considered extinct in 1950. They were reintroduced in Canada by hunters and now number over one hundred thousand.

Income from licences, permits, and tags—$12.5 million.

Jobs (estimated)—4,200 person years

Reference: Ontario Ministry of Natural Resources (MNR) and Ontario Federation of Anglers and Hunters (OFAH)

I have not found income data derived from small game and migratory bird hunting (ducks, geese, partridge, pheasants, rabbits, groundhogs to name a few). Gathering data is difficult. Revenue from licences goes to the federal government. Contributed income from small game hunting is conservatively estimated at over $20 million.

Deer population is increasing so rapidly in Ontario, particularly in Southern and Northwestern Ontario, that accurate population figures are difficult to acquire. However, because of the tremendous increase observed by farmers, biologists, forest managers, and some conservation organizations, the Ministry of Natural Resources is being urged to issue more deer tags to increase the number harvested. They are concerned about the growing amount of damage that deer are doing to crops, trees, and destroying habitat other species need for their existence.

More details are provided in chapter 3, "Benefits of Hunting."

*   *   *

Many who have antihunting leanings are not aware of the foregoing information and the support it lends to hunting as a worthy endeavour. There are also some who, despite this and other such evidence, remain antihunting advocates. I think there is a need for a greater awareness and appreciation of the foregoing data but also of other important benefits provided by the hunting experience. Some benefits are not so obvious.

Sometimes, I feel a bit like Louis Armstrong when he was asked to explain jazz. He replied, "If you have to ask, ain't nothin' I can say gonna help." He also said, "There are some people that if they don't know, you can't tell 'em." Nevertheless, I have had some success in creating a better understanding of hunting, so I shall forge ahead.

For me, hunting has always been a metaphor for life. During the journey, there are enjoyable, beautiful, inspirational times and challenging and unpleasant times as well as much mystery in the entire process. In my experience, life blossoms when the mysterious ways in which the world works are viewed with reverence. I am fully aware that there will be resistance in some quarters to many of the ideas set forth in this book. There are as many controversial and disturbing aspects in hunting as there are in life itself. I find that people can become quite emotional about such topics, and getting beyond one's way of thinking and overcoming prejudices can be difficult. An opinion that differs from one's own can be irritating. But we should not use this to dismiss discussions or attempt to avoid them. Certainly, there are imperfections in every endeavour in life. However, it seems to me that searching for the good in anything and then encouraging individuals in that direction makes most sense in the long run.

*   *   *

In years gone by, the native elders initiated youths into adulthood through hunting. From this experience, youths gained valuable insights into the flow of life, a reverence for and a bond with all things in the universe. They gained self-confidence, a sense of personal responsibility towards themselves and towards others. They learned the importance of hard work, how to handle adversity, and the wisdom of going with the flow of life instead of fighting against what life is trying to offer.

Have you ever pondered about the old proverb "If you want to learn about life, go down to the river and watch"?

* * *

Has the world between *then* and *now* changed all that radically? Are there lessons from the past that offer insights that could help us today? And are such lessons still obtainable? Are there relationships between our civilized self, our authentic self, our animal self, and everything else in the world? Are there experiences capable of engendering a feeling of awe—a condition that many sages say is the beginning of wisdom? I suspect there are; however, there are also anomalies and mysterious elements that make it extremely difficult to easily explain.

David Cumes, MD, in his book on wilderness healing and discovery of self points out that, as many others have, we are not that far removed from our hunter-gatherer ancestry and that buried in our psyche are hunter-gatherer forces. He advocates wilderness experience for the discovery of self and healing—and the more we approximate the hunter-gatherer model, the more we will discover the spiritual and self-actualizing benefit of the experience. Of course, the consequences to the wild outdoors need to be taken into account. In one chapter, Cumes details how he learned by watching and participating with the !Kung San hunter-gatherers in Africa as they carefully made and set their traps, even for smaller animals (when larger animals were scarce), then skinned the little creatures in preparation for their various uses of all the parts.

Robert Bly in his best-selling book *Iron John* makes a powerful call for a return to the hunting initiation as a means of reducing many of societies' ills.

The June 2000 issue of *North American Hunter*, the world's largest outdoor magazine, reports that proper initiation in hunting can curb teen violence. Written by Dr. Randall Eaton, a scientific authority on animal behaviour and on the role hunting has played in behavioural evolution, the article points out, as did Bly, that hunting was the traditional way of initiating young men into adulthood and, when properly done, is still the best way to get them properly connected to the world around us.

Perhaps the foregoing ideas deserve greater consideration. Many people are not coping well with life.

How to cope successfully with the harsh situations that occur in life has to be taught or learned. As much as we all wish for a world in which only pleasantries exist, this is not reality.

> *If you want your children to have a peaceful life, let them*
> *suffer a little hunger and a little coldness.*
>
> —Chinese proverb

The preeminent Swiss psychologist and psychiatrist Carl Jung contributed immensely to our understanding of human behaviour and to ways for alleviating behavioural problems. He is quoted as complaining that modern people too often get their experiences from words and dictionaries to such an extent that they are surprised when they meet up with a real cow and actually experience its smell. They are unprepared for the full reality of a "cow." To know a cow is to experience a cow—not read about one. Implicit in this metaphor is that by not engaging in real experiences, one is vulnerable to flawed thinking about many things in life. This, says Jung, often causes frustrations that contribute to psychological and physical health problems—a concept that is explored in detail in this book.

*   *   *

I have come to believe that urbanization contributes to various problems in our society, often in ways that are not at all obvious or easily proven. My thesis is that city living has disconnected us, even alienated us, from the way in which the natural world works. City design is such that the natural world is all but blocked out. The realities of the food chain and the flow or cycle of life are hidden from us, leaving a space—a vacuum if you will—that allows and indeed encourages unrealistic expectations. This is a fertile field for the growth of unhappiness and stressful feelings, which, in turn, are significant contributors to increased anger, violence, crime, and ill health. Violence and crime are further exacerbated by video games that dramatize violence and create a false perspective of life and death. In these games, there is no moral consequence to destroying something; in fact, you are rewarded. So when in real life the person becomes frustrated, instead of working it out in a constructive way, he or she is more likely to respond with a violent act. There is a growing body of evidence that supports such claims, so when I bounce these ideas off my friends, I usually get nods of agreement. Many of my friends, however, particularly those born and raised in cities, frequently question what I call the "disconnection from nature" or dispute my claim that hunting experiences can alleviate many problems.

In this document, I cite personal experiences from time to time, not to indulge myself but in hope that they lend authenticity to the opinions expressed. I hope you will find my vignettes and perspectives interesting as well as food for thought.

A generally accepted principle is that what one learns in a particular endeavour spills over into other areas. I believe that some of my observations and comments illustrate this. For instance, one offshoot from my hunting education is that I tend to watch for the signs and tracks made by individuals, governments, and organizations—signs that indicate the direction headed. I am deeply interested in the politics of our democracy. Examples I relate relative to hunting are important and cautionary signals about political approaches. Similar to "the tip of the iceberg," the approaches to which I refer give a warning sign of greater underlying menace. Too often, actions are motivated unduly by self-serving considerations and without sensible reflection on the possible long-term side effects that can negate the original intent. Consequently, I have included thoughts on some practices that warrant closer scrutiny. The situations described are not unique to Canada. After all, there are similar trends worldwide. Democracy is not a spectator sport.

Some reviewers suggest that my book concentrates on the joys and benefits of hunting along with my stories and that my comments on peripheral issues be minimized. Certainly, the former are important and, for some readers, may be enough. However, I find my observations have significance not only for hunting issues but for others as well. On occasion, negative reactions to hunting have been softened through discussions of apparent inconsistencies in life, including processes in politics, so I have included a few pertinent thoughts about them. Some of you may want to skim over parts in which you have little interest. However, I hope you will at least accept the possibility of their significance. Perhaps some of you will want to reread sections. With this in my mind and because of the way chapters developed, similar to essays, some points are repeated. In the sections where this occurs, the repeated perspectives are important to the specific topic.

You Never Know

You never know when someone
May catch a dream from you.
You never know when a little word,
Or something you may do
May open up a window
Of the mind that seeks the light.
The way you live may not matter at all,
But you never know . . . it might.
And just in case it could be
That another's life through you,
Might possibly change for the better
With a broader, brighter view.
It seems it might be worth a try
At pointing the way to the right,
Of course, it may not matter at all
But then again . . . it might. (Author unknown)

*   *   *

In discussions with people about hunting, I have found that appealing to their sensibilities by comparing paradoxical portraits helps create a more open and favourable perspective on hunting—for instance, likening the pros and cons of hunting to the good and bad aspects of other things such as religion, sport, or sex. For those of you who are interested in exploring more thoughts relative to paradoxes, turn to chapter 16, "Life Is a Paradox." Some of you may find reading that section now is worthwhile before proceeding.

*   *   *

Events occur in nature that may appear tragic or cruel in human terms. I believe this perception is a result of something not understood. It is an undesirable attitude for the simple reason that if nature is perceived as cruel that negativism tends to permeate into a person's general interpretation of life's challenges. This, in turn, can result in much unnecessary unhappiness. A more positive attitude or interpretation can make a world of difference. Les Brown, the American author and motivational speaker, expresses this thought, "Don't let the negativity given to you by the world disempower you. Instead, give to yourself that which empowers you."

Chief Dan George's words come to mind: what you don't know you fear, and what you fear you destroy. It happens so often and in so many ways. Psychologists, psychiatrists, and human potential trainers caution us about the negative outcomes that such fears bring to us. They express the idea in many different ways, for example,

> *Fear is the most devastating of all emotions.*
> *Fear poisons the body.*
> *One oppresses what one fears.*
> *What you fear you attract into your life.*

Although there is a negative aspect to fear, on the other hand, we all recognize that fear has a legitimate and worthy place in human nature. Without it, we would not survive for long. It keeps us out of the jaws of harm. It is part of the fight-or-flight response. However, some like to use the word "cautious" in place of fear because fear has such an insidious way of gravitating towards detrimental fear.

Detrimental fear is really an exaggerated fear or an irrational fear that we have been taught. It is a fear that we cling to long after its purpose has been served. Often these are, or have become, subconscious fears. Peak potential trainers and psychologists refer to fear as a nasty emotion and as all too common in our society. They point to the many ways in which fear takes over our thoughts and bodies and immobilizes us. Fear often happens when we peer into the future and focus on possible problems that may or may not happen. Fear is one reason why some individuals avoid hunting and wilderness experiences and why they discourage others from participating.

There are events that occur in hunting where caution (normal fear) is necessary, but there is no place for exaggerated fear. Hunting has the potential to reduce detrimental fears and restore a healthy, balanced perspective. A paradox, I suggest.

*   *   *

The primal human being perceived the natural world as rich with meaning. Spirits were seen in the forest; presences were felt in the wind, rivers, and mountains. Meaning was recognized in birds and animals and in the cycle of sun, moon, and planets. Leaders perpetuated these ideas with stories and initiations that gave youths the perspectives that helped them manage situations in the world in which *they* lived.

When a person experiences nature in a wilderness setting, there is often an awakening to the marvellous, mysterious functioning of this spinning planet in which humans are but one cog, albeit a special one. It is a mind-boggling experience yet somehow soothes the soul and engenders a space where contentment can be found. Various feelings and thoughts can surface while sitting quietly when hunting or later when contemplating the events of a hunt or wondering about the act of taking a creature's life.

*   *   *

I have been concerned for some time that many of my urban friends carry an unfavourable image of hunting. I am also concerned about their lack of basic knowledge about modern-day wildlife management and nature's flow of life. I am even more worried about the increasing spread of negative perceptions of hunting that are spread through advertising, the news media, television shows, and books—ideas that are prompting our governments to pass laws under the guise of democracy, laws that tend to squeeze the life out of hunting. The ambivalence of the majority of voters allows this to happen. I suggest this is an improper and misleading path. Hunting has an important place in our society.

Perhaps hunters should be considered stewards though not all hunters will accept this responsibility or are able to articulate the deep meaning that hunting has for them. But this is true for many people in many walks of life. The life of a gardener is possibly the most appropriate metaphor with which to communicate the nature of a steward. Metaphorically, he has to roll up his sleeves and bury his hands in the dirt to fully participate in caring for his crop.

*   *   *

People discourage hunting for various reasons, often the result of opinions passed on by parents and others that are accepted without personal inquiry. One underlying factor, I find, is that many people do not want to see the perceived pain in the process of taking a life, even when it is for food. Although we may not like pain, it exists and is part of nature and is inherent in the food chain. Many philosophers and spiritual leaders point out that, in addition to being a warning signal, pain is an aspect that can teach us to be more human, understanding, and humble. This poses a quandary for most of us. I have been able to gain respect for the methods of our Creator, which has made this dilemma easier for me to accept. The basis for my opinions should become clearer upon reading my stories and comments in the following sections of this document.

Hunting exposes the participant to the reality of life and death as well as other aspects in the flow of life, which helps one in coping with quandaries. Hunting nurtures an appreciation of nature's system where one species must kill for another to survive and where without predators creatures tend to overproduce and cause their own demise. The overall experience has an uncanny way of alleviating many frustrations, especially when mentored maturely. I hope to be able to illustrate this in the following pages.

CHAPTER 3

Benefits of hunting

The following data, mostly for Ontario, is used here because it is fittingly illustrative. Ontario is a large diverse province with twelve million people and an area covering one million square kilometres—twice the area of France, bigger than Germany, 1.4 times larger than Texas.

- According to the most recent survey in 1996, *The Importance of Nature to Canadians*, there were 314,000 hunters in Ontario. Big game hunters alone spent $200.6 million annually on hunting wildlife ($16 million in taxes). This data does not include small game, turkey, duck, partridge, and pheasant hunters or the activities of the 141,525 aboriginals who live here.
- Hunting provides much-needed jobs for outfitters, guides, and supporting services—estimated to be equivalent to 4,200 person years. Many more than this number of persons are employed because the activities are seasonal. It is difficult to determine exact numbers though sixteen thousand is considered a reasonable estimate. These jobs are especially significant because they are mainly in high-unemployment, low-income areas.
- In Ontario from 2000 to 2004, some 2.4 million hunting licences were sold. This does not include permits to hunt migratory birds, which the federal government sells. In Ontario, deer and moose hunters paid $10 million in licence fees in 2004.
- Some 70 percent to 80 percent of the total operating budget for Ontario's wildlife and fisheries programs (enforcing, research,

stocking, monitoring) comes from hunting and fishing revenues of which hunting is the major portion by far.

- A survey by Environment Canada in 1996 found that hunters invested $65 million in contributions between 1984 and 1999 to support wildlife. This is in addition to that spent directly in hunting activities. During the same period, volunteers logged ten million hours helping restore wildlife habitat.

- Hunters provide their wildlife control services mostly free to the taxpayer. In the absence of public hunting or trapping, government would likely be called upon to step in and control wildlife to some degree. Based on a survey of state wildlife agencies and available literature, the potential cost of government-run agencies in Canada are as follows:

1. Approximately $17 million to $34 million in annual expenditures is needed to remove problem furbearers.
2. An amount of $35.7 million annually is needed for crop and livestock damages.
3. Payouts for wildlife-auto collisions would be significantly higher. There is growing concern about current costs. In Manitoba, for example, payouts for wildlife-auto collisions averaged $20 per resident in 2003.

- Hunters are the prime impetus behind wildlife management. This entails controlling wildlife overpopulation and ensuring the sustainability of the resource. They are also the driving force behind wildlife reintroductions such as elk and wild turkey in Ontario. The same group is a major force in restocking lakes with fish and working to protect endangered species. The tremendous increases in wildlife in North America have been mainly the result of funds and resources provided by hunters. In Ontario in the past ten years, wild turkey have gone from 0 to over 30,000; deer from 100,000 to over 350,000; moose from 80,000 to 114,000; ducks and geese have increased substantially; and the bear population has risen to over 100,000. Not a single wildlife species in Ontario is declining because of hunting says Dr. Terry Quinney, provincial coordinator of Fish and Wildlife Services.

- Hunting provides meat—about twelve million pounds from sustainable herds in Ontario each year. It is considered by many to be more nutritious and tasty than commercial products.
- Hunter safety training has made hunting one of the safest outdoor activities, a fact seldom recognized by the antihunting lobby or by journalists. The compulsory training required to obtain a permit to own a firearm and the further training required to obtain a hunting licence are far more extensive than that required for a licence to drive a car. In addition, many gun and hunting clubs provide safety training. Dr. Quinney points out that according to the National Safety Council, hunting is safer than golf, horseback riding, bicycling, baseball, swimming, and boating. Lightning is twenty times the danger.

   The following benefits are difficult to quantify but nonetheless are very real.
- Hunting is a healthy recreation that has many of the elements of all good sports—teamwork, exercise, excitement, goals, and challenge.
- Hunting teaches responsibility and valuable perspectives on life and death. The whole experience provides one with the opportunity to analyze their relationship on this planet. There is blood, and there is death. To witness it can bring about some blunt, stimulating truths about the mysterious ways in which the world works. For many hunters, their first kill is a transformational experience. It is an awakening for them that often leads to a newfound reverence for life. New hunters become very aware of the deathly capabilities of the tool in their hands.
- Hunting provides an outlet for an instinct that is as old as man. It is a psychological tenet that to deny an instinct is risky because it then surfaces frequently in inappropriate ways or inhibits valuable attributes such as positive aggression and creativity.
- The following expresses a subtle value in hunting that is illustrative of many hunters' feelings. A woman from Southwestern Ontario wrote,

   Hunting for me is not only a way of putting meat on the table, but rather a very big part of who I am as a person. I would have to say that hunting is one of the largest contributing factors to the closeness of my family . . . when I am sitting there quietly; I also have time to think. I think of my past, present and future. I think of things that make me happy and sad. It's like meditation for me . . .

One day I got a call from my sister who was dying of cancer and she said there was something very important she needed to talk to me about. She said "You know how you've told me you have time to think over your life when you are hunting? Well I was thinking that as long as you keep hunting—you will think of me. I'm guaranteed my immortality with you. I know that while you are sitting there quietly I will come into your thoughts. That is how I will have my immortality with you more than anyone else.

Shortly after my sister's funeral, I went moose hunting. I had a whole week in the care and company of friends, with plenty of time to sit by myself in the bush and think. After that I spent a week deer hunting. Those two weeks accomplished more for my mental health than thousands of dollars of therapy ever could have.

I will miss my sister for the rest of my life. But I know as long as I can go hunting there will be a time when she is with me.

I hope this helps you better understand how hunting is not just something I do, but is a very big part of who I am as a person. It connects me to the food I eat. It connects me to my sister. And to lose hunting would be to lose all that.

CHAPTER 4

My boyhood hunting experiences

I have never climbed Mount Everest or canoed the wild white water of the Nahanni River, but some of my hunting experiences created similar feelings in me.

At what age did I start hunting? Probably from day one, but I will start my stories with tadpoles.

HUNTING FOR TADPOLES

A new pond in the suburbs of our town was created by highway construction. This pond became a haven for little green frogs. In the spring of the year, a chorus of hundreds of chirping "creepers" filled the balmy twilight. When I was six, I went to observe these frogs and explore in the muddy water in bare feet and rolled-up pants. Some little "creatures" bumped into my bare legs. I made a dip net with my handkerchief and scooped in the water, catching clumps of frog eggs and tiny tadpoles. It was great excitement to see how many tadpoles I could catch. I returned a few days later with a bigger roughly crafted dip net and a bucket to hold captured tadpoles, which I later transferred to a bigger tub in our backyard. Most of them died, some bursting from overeating the bread and oatmeal that I threw too generously into the water. Some survived, and I observed them in various stages of development—their tails disappearing and tiny feet sprouting from their plump little bodies.

HUNTING FOR BIRDS' EGGS

Birds of various species were very plentiful in the town and surrounding countryside. There were thousands, some of which were pests in the gardens and fields. Why not make a collection of birds' eggs? The mother birds would not miss one egg, similar to a chicken, I rationalized. So my buddies and I started collecting birds' eggs and competing to see who could collect the most types. We made holes in the ends of the eggs by gently inserting a pin then blowing out the innards, leaving the shells. We spent hours tramping through the fields, swamps, and woods looking for different birds and their nests—on the ground, in the holes of telephone poles made by woodpeckers, in bulrushes, on the water, and high up in trees (which required some tough, risky climbing and wading). I sometimes regret that the collection was thrown out. Looking at the various eggs now would add details to such wonderful memories.

BLACKBIRD EVENT

One day when I was ten, my buddy and I went hunting with our BB guns, looking for starlings and blackbirds—species that were considered pests. But they were too smart for us and flew off whenever we crept within shooting range. Finally, I snuck up on one high in a tree, took aim, and pulled the trigger. He dropped to the ground, dead. I scooped him up and marched proceeding to the stable and displayed my great marksmanship to my uncle. He looked at the dead bird, grinned at me, and said, "You've shot a female robin. Best you don't let your aunt see it."

My heart sank. How could I have been so careless? I did not want to kill a robin nor did I want to displease my aunt. I have been more careful ever since.

A SUCCESSFUL BULLFROG HUNT: AGE ELEVEN

Someone mentioned that bullfrog legs were a delicacy served in the finest restaurants in France. So we decided to try them. First, we had to find and catch bullfrogs, but none existed as far north as the area where I lived. However, I had heard them croaking at my uncle's cottage located one hundred kilometres south. So on a visit there, I took my BB gun, and my older cousin took a .22 rifle. We climbed into a boat and paddled around lily pads hunting bullfrogs. We shot and retrieved thirty of them, making sure they were dead before cutting off their legs. See below a picture of a string of frog legs. My aunt cooked the legs with a bit of difficulty because the legs kept twitching and jumping about in the frying pan. We enjoyed a delicious meal of frog legs, one that has never been surpassed. The frog legs I ate years later in a café in Paris, France, didn't come close.

Left to right: Cousin Ken, brothers Ron, Ralph,
John with frogs' legs.

HUNTING WITH MY MOTHER

My father passed away when I was six. He had been a farmer and hunter and had left a couple of rifles, one of which was a Remington pump action .22. I discovered it hidden in a cubbyhole and loved to fondle and play with it in the confines of my bedroom. Eventually, I began to sneak it out of the house to go hunting and target shooting in the bush by the river. To transport and hide the rifle for this illegal act as I walked through town to the seclusion of the bush, I separated the rifle into two sections and stuffed each down a pant leg. To hold the sections from sliding to the ground, each was tied to an end of a short length of fishing line that I strung around the back of my neck and over my shoulders.

When I was twelve, an uncle asked Mother if it would be acceptable for him to give "the boys" some bullets for the .22. He advised her that his short low-powered bullets were ideal for shooting partridge. He advised Mother that he thought we were very mature for our age. I suspect he knew that I was already using the gun. My mother talked to us about gun safety and warned us that if she ever found us misusing the privilege, she would be very hurt. She also assigned us the job of cleaning the stable and harnessing the horses. Is it really fair to have to shovel manure to carry a gun? Sometimes, I wonder; but in my heart, I knew that with freedom came responsibility. At least, I know that now.

To my surprise, my mother allowed us to accept the bullets and to use the gun. On several occasions, she joined us for a walk on clear, frosty fall days while we hunted for partridge. We wandered across pastures and along bush roads and trails, enjoying the beauty of autumn colours and the general ambience of the surroundings. She took great pleasure in these outings. Occasionally, we were startled by the loud whir of a flushed partridge. Sometimes, one of us heard one or caught a glimpse of one eating on the ground or in a tree or sitting on a stump. The detection caused us to stop immediately and be very quiet as I crept within shooting range of the bird, took aim, and fired. After a few hours, we trudged home with several partridge in hand and a very proud mother.

While we cleaned the partridge and prepared vegetables, Mother made pies—apple and pumpkin were her specialty. The evening meal of partridge, fried or stewed, followed by pie topped with whipped cream was always a grand occasion. We retired early—relaxed, thankful, and happy.

Bob Beach's wood carving of a partridge.

There were many outings with mother that had similar effects. Although each was somewhat different in makeup, they all fostered an affinity with nature and kindled feelings of well-being. A walk in the wilderness in the spring after the snow had disappeared was an invigorating event. At this time of year many things come alive after the long winter. We observed the regeneration process of nature: the new leaves on the shrubs and trees, the budding ferns, the numerous species of birds that had returned from the south and were now busily preparing to nest, the beautiful wild flowers, and the warmth and freshness in the gentle breeze. Below is a photo of mother's favourite wildflower, the rarely found lady-slippers that she so enjoyed, and another photo of her relaxing at our remote cottage.

Lady-slippers   Mother relaxing

Sighs Are the Springs Of Life

It's an early April wind
That gusts at autumn's remnants
Now molded from winter's grave.
The breeze is sometimes playful
Tossing its dead captives about
On their grey-green graves.
Now anxious, as if to replace
The lifeless leaves to tomb-like
Trees. Now pensive—surveying
Its vain attempt at revival.
And the sun's rays having spent
Their warming support, settle with
The sighing April air.

Joan Gibbins (author's wife)

RABBIT EPISODE

I will never forget a midwinter hunting incident when I was twelve. We were living in the country where my mother had taken a teaching position in a one-room school. As I mentioned above, I was allowed to hunt with a pump action .22 rifle that had belonged to my father; and one sunny, cold winter day, we decided a tasty rabbit stew would warm us up. There were plenty of rabbit tracks in the surrounding bush. So off we went. But the rabbits that made those tracks were nowhere to be seen. I recall being told about an old Swedish bush worker whose only tool was an axe but who nonetheless was often seen trudging home with a rabbit for dinner. When asked how he managed to catch them, he replied, "When rabbit go in bush pile, me go in too."

So I looked around for bush piles. Sure enough, I spotted one—with a big white rabbit sitting on top basking in the sun, barely discernible in the snow. I took aim and fired. The rabbit flipped into the air and cried like a baby before succumbing.

That scene disturbed me as it probably has you. My younger brother was quite shaken. I wondered why. We had shot partridge without it bothering us and had cut the heads of flapping, struggling chickens. We had witnessed animals killed for food and the squeal of a pig in the throes of death. But because we had pet rabbits, the cry from that rabbit had affected us differently. We also had a cat and a dog. We had trained them not to harm our rabbits. The dog never went near them, but the cat would occasionally sleep with them in the old horse stable. The cat would also kill and drag home a wild rabbit. I recall wondering about the inconsistencies.

I noticed too that one of my uncles couldn't kill a calf he had raised, or my grandfather a lamb. They got someone else to do the deed. But they could hunt and kill wild animals. Obviously, people and animals can and do form attachments. We need to be on guard against making erroneous decisions based on this. Recently, I became aware of another situation that I suspect illustrates what I am discussing here. I have been communicating with biologists who have been studying black bears for years and issues relative to hunting them. Most of these biologists don't hunt bears. They seem to have developed an attachment to bears but support the bear hunt for conservation, population control, and social and economic values that go hand in hand with the bear hunt.

I can recall thinking at one point in time that it would be a more humane world if we had evolved in a way that enabled us to survive on water for our food. I have read about a group advocating this very idea. However, on further thought, I came to the realization that even water contains all kinds of living organisms that we kill when we purify and drink water.

MY OWLS, CROWS, AND HAWKS

The following is the text of the first speech I gave at a Toastmasters club that I joined to learn and practice public speaking. I was forty at the time and living in Toronto. As an attention getter, I opened my talk by imitating the strange sounds of a startled great horned owl when he is frightened and retaliates by threatening to bite with his sharp beak by opening and closing it rapidly with a loud snapping sound. And he hisses. The *snap snap snap hiss* sound I made can't be adequately conveyed here. You'll have to accept my word. It got immediate attention.

I continued the speech saying, "Now what in the world is that? Well, by the time I am finished with this talk, you will know it represents excitement, adventure, and a boyhood learning experience. I was fourteen at the time, and my young brother was eleven."

It was a bright, sunny spring day. The leaves were just starting to bud. The air had a crisp freshness unknown to our polluted cities. My young brother, our dog, and I meandered through the fields and woods, watching for wildlife and in particular birds' nests. We finally came to the river, swollen and swift from the winter's runoff of snow and ice.

We sat down on a log for lunch. I looked up into the clear blue sky and soaked up contentment that only nature can produce. And then I spotted it, high in an almost branchless tree—a giant bird's nest; or is it just a cluster of old leaves and branches? I wondered. It had definite form, so it must be a nest. But what kind of bird would build such a huge nest? I could not imagine.

I immediately knew that I had to have a look in that nest. But how to climb the big almost-branchless tree? There was only one way, and that was to shinny up. So I started clawing my way up, clinging to the rough bark with fingers and knees.

Suddenly, a huge bird appeared overhead. It seemed to darken the sky with a gigantic wingspan of about six feet. So this was the builder of the nest, and it was obviously disturbed.

Though sensing danger, I was determined to reach that nest to add a great horned owl's egg to my collection. With my brother as lookout, I continued climbing cautiously. It was an opportunity of a lifetime.

Our dog, a large Brittany spaniel, was swimming across the narrow swift-flowing river below. The great horned owl reappeared from nowhere, gliding silently down towards the dog, almost grabbing him with his huge claws. An owl can't see well in the daylight, but this didn't deter this one. He turned and swooped again, coming even closer to the dog.

"Call the dog back!" I yelled at my brother. "Or he will be torn to shreds!"

But the dog sensed the danger and swam as fast as he could to reach the shelter of the trees, and my brother said in a shaky voice, "Don't you think you should come down?"

His fear made me more determined.

"Hang on to the dog and warn me when the owl comes near me!" I shouted.

I started to climb again. The big owl kept reappearing overhead, swooping lower and lower towards me, and I was getting higher and higher with less and less protection.

I was just below the nest now; and as I eased my chin up over the edge of the nest, I came face-to-face with a snapping, hissing beak! I ducked quickly under the nest, caught my breath, and announced, "The old girl is sitting on her eggs."

I dared not poke my unprotected face over the edge again, so I broke an old branch from the tree that was covered with animal hair and partially digested bones that had been spit out by the owls. I reached up trying to nudge what I thought was the mother off her eggs. My efforts were frequently interrupted with the ever-dangerous owl swooping overhead trying to focus its eyes on the intruder for an all-out attack.

A big bird suddenly appeared at the edge of the nest. I instinctively pushed it with the stick, thinking it was the mother. It fell, flapping its wings as it tumbled to the ground.

Well, I'll be darned; it's a baby great horned owl, I concluded. I eased my head up to investigate the interior of the nest and was met with another snapping, hissing beak. With my stick, I tenderly pushed it out, and it fluttered to the ground. I then had a good look in the nest and saw the remains of their food. I detected bits of rabbit, mouse, squirrel, and other birds. I slithered down the tree, relieved to be free from the danger overhead.

I grabbed the packsack.

"What are you going to do now?" my brother asked.

"I'm going to catch those young owls, take them home, and raise them for pets," I replied.

In a short time, we had rounded up the two owls, which were over twelve inches tall and predominantly claws, snapping beaks, and feathers. We managed to stuff them side by side, feet first, into the packsack. With them on my back, we started home.

On the way, we spotted two more nests. Of course, I had to climb the trees to have a look. A vicious hawk circled one, and an angry crow the other. There were no eggs but three young ones in each. I resolved to come back later for more pets.

We were very proud and very excited with our accomplishment and immediately set about preparing a place to keep them. Now what to call them? Those were the days of radio, and the sounds of the popular program *The Adventures of Ozzie and Harriet* drifted out an open window. Ozzie and Harriet—perfect names for the owls!

Ozzie and Harriet thrived and grew on a diet of scrap bones from the butcher shop and trapped mice. They ate everything and anything. I marvelled at their digestive system. They became quite an attraction, and the kids in the neighbourhood flocked to feed and observe them.

Photo of great horned owl.

We also had a couple of rabbits, a crow, and three little hawks from the nests mentioned above. I had made three trips to the hawk nest, waiting for them to be robust enough to survive my less-than-perfect parenting. The mother hawk appeared to have abandoned her young prior to my last visit, so I adopted all three.

I had a pet crow the prior year named Oscar. He was an interesting character who became very attached to the family but fell into the rain barrel while taking a bath one day and drowned. So the new crow became Oscar. I could not decide on names for the hawks. I marvelled at their little bright eyes and obvious intelligence.

The owls were unique creatures with unbelievable characteristics. They had a wonderful digestive system. There was no need to chew their food—a mouse, dead or alive, went down with one gulp. Bones and hair were spit out later. If some fool threw cigarettes into their gapping mouths, down they would go. Their strong beaks and large claws were capable of tearing a rabbit apart for a quick lunch, so we were careful to keep our pet rabbits away from them. To watch their huge pupils expand and contract as they tried to focus was fascinating. When one of our owls managed to get loose and perched in the open, all kinds of birds including crows, swallows, blackbirds, and starlings appeared from nowhere in squadrons to dive at him like attacking Spitfires. The owls were evidently feared and hated by all the other birds and animals. Even my big dog kept his distance as did the cats. The owls displayed little affection towards me, not like the crow and hawks did, but demonstrated some recognition and trust in me.

One day, the town policeman, old Bill McPherson, marched in and said, "I have had some complaints. You are not allowed to keep wild animals and must get rid of them, or I will."

I promised that I would do what was necessary. I felt that by releasing the owls in the woods by the river on Grandmother's farm, I could gradually wean them. They were big and strong—about two feet tall with wingspans of over five feet. I had been considering letting them go anyway, so this is what I did. The young hawks were not capable of surviving on their own, so when I fed them their last supper to close their big begging mouths, I tapped each one lightly on the head with a hammer, and they peacefully slipped away. Oscar was a different matter. I knew that if I took him to the woods, he would just follow me home. I hated the thought but knew I had to put him away. With a light tap to his head, Oscar too met his maker.

"HOW CRUEL!" is the reaction of many people. Thank goodness for such a reaction. It is the same quality that makes us sensitive, considerate, and nurturing. But it is important to go beyond that initial feeling, to a deeper understanding of nature, life, and death. To me, what I did was similar to killing the chickens for food. It was something that had to be done. It was part of life, and without death, there is no life. We can stick our head in the sand but are then subject to a kick in the butt and missing possible nurturing energies available to a position of openness.

A scientific maxim is that energy is never lost—it simply changes form. For example, burnt wood changes to heat, gases, and nutrients. The new physics says all matter is living—a tenet of gurus for centuries. I know that the bodies of my little friends returned to Mother Earth to provide nourishment for other species. It also seems reasonable to assume that their spirits went somewhere.

Many young people enjoyed and learned from my little zoo.

It is a psychological tenet that we need good memories to balance ourselves. Those who do not have good memories often have to learn to develop them to achieve a happier state. I am thankful for my memories. The experience was also a lesson for me in personal responsibility and tough love, two very important ingredients in managing life successfully.

On returning for a holiday several years after I left home, I heard that an unusually large owl had been shot on my grandmother's farm. I made inquiries and determined that the incident happened very close to the spot where I had released Ozzie and Harriet. I knew the fate of at least one of them. I also heard that other great horned owls had been seen along the river—descendents I am sure.

CHAPTER 5

A boyhood hunting tragedy and a lesson:
the shooting of Custard

One autumn when I was twelve, three friends and I paddled by canoe up a narrow river to a log cabin we had built. We had slingshots to practice shooting and with which we hoped to bag a partridge or two. On our way home, the four of us were gliding in the canoe down river in a fast-flowing current. I was in the stern steering the canoe. All of a sudden, we saw splashes near us in the water and heard rifle shots. On the high steep bank overlooking the river stood three teenage partridge hunters, laughing and shooting into the water to scare us. The bullet from the last shot put five holes in Custard, one of my buddies who was sitting in the bottom of the canoe. The bullet went in and out of his calf, in and out of his inner thigh, and into his scrotum. The canoe teetered when he slumped to one side, screaming in pain. I managed to steady the canoe and steered to shore. We pulled up on shore and made Custard as comfortable as possible. The three teenagers, thankfully, ran into town to get the doctor who arrived about two hours later. Luckily, no permanent damage was done.

The court case drew a lot of attention. A district judge from another town presided. The town hall was packed with spectators. Although only twelve at the time, I was called to testify. No one knew for sure who had fired that last shot.

Addressing the court, one father expressed his disappointment with his son's behaviour, explaining how he had spent a great deal of time with his son teaching him to properly use a gun and to hunt responsibly. He apologized for his failure with his son and for what had happened. Another father who was not a hunter attempted to challenge the police investigation. He said that his investigation showed that the bullet could not have come from the boys because of the angle of penetration and suggested the bullet was probably a stray from someone else nearby.

In his summation, the judge commented that sometimes, boys misbehave even with good parenting and suggested that the one father could learn from the other's example. The judge said that in his assessment, the bullet had indeed come from the gun of the boy whose father said his son could not have done it. This boy was given a longer suspended sentence than that given to the other boys, and all three received a stern lecture on responsible behaviour. It was never suggested by anyone that it was wrong for teenagers to have guns. Their behaviour was punished, and they learned a valuable lesson. I am sure that the experience helped them become more considerate and careful in other areas of their lives. It was also a wake-up call for many others.

Most people today, including members of Parliament, seem obsessed with attaching blame to the gun; and more and more gun control laws are being passed to try to control their misuse. The gun has become a menace as if it is to blame. I know many who will not allow a firearm in their house. To my way of thinking, this is akin to blaming the car when someone gets killed or injured by one or blaming liquor when it is misused. Teaching individuals the dangers of misuse and how to be responsible and enjoy the activity has the greatest chance of success by far. This is true for many things—alcohol, cars, and sex to name a few.

The subject of gun control will be discussed in detail in following chapters for several reasons. We are all very concerned about the criminal use of guns and what is or is not effective in current methods that attempt to curb it as well as the negative impacts of some prescribed solutions.

CHAPTER 6

More hunting experiences

Occasionally, I am asked to describe what a hunt is like. There is such a variety in the types of hunting, the associated camps, and hunting experiences that it is almost impossible to give justice to the subject. The following, however, are a couple of examples of my experiences that have meaning for me and a few others, so maybe they will for you too.

Hunters love to tell stories. It is part and parcel of the hunting experience. In the evening around the fire, we enjoy relating our experiences with animals and about life. Through stories, we get to know one another. Stories entertain as well as educate. We learn from the tales told. In fact, man is a story-telling animal.

There are many subjects discussed at a hunt camp in addition to the specifics of hunting. Politics, world events, people, sex, cars, and previous hunting experiences are all fair game.

A HUNT WITH OLD-TIMERS: *A Story That Reveals Bits about the Past and Characteristics of the Hunting Spirit*

In 1953, I was working long hours in the Montreal area; but at the age of twenty-three, had plenty of energy and felt the urge to hunt. So I headed north and met Uncle Jim at Englehart, and we headed up the lake to his camp. It was Saturday, and after my long drive (750 kilometres) and a delicious meal of stew and fresh bread, I was tired and about to bunk down early.

It was a cold, miserable, rainy evening as black as pitch when, all of a sudden, there was a loud thump on the door; and in walked Arnold Shortt,

Bert Tardiff, and Arthur Margueratt. In the dim light of the flickering coal oil lamp, they looked like the proverbial drowned rats—big ugly ones at that. Bert—a tall, large-framed man with his bushy moustache and large-brimmed black hat—was an imposing hulk in the small one-room cabin. The others were not as large but scruffy looking in the shadows with their soaking wet wool garb.

They were frequent visitors on the lake during hunting season; and on Saturdays, after Arnold finished his shift at a mine in Kirkland Lake, Uncle's recently built log cabin was a haven to them. In those days, they hunted in a valley over a high hill they called the mountain. It was a three-quarter-mile, four-hundred-foot steep climb to the top—a slippery one at that—followed by a trek of about a mile and a half east to their hunting grounds. They called it the Big Valley. There were no access roads to the valley then and no snow machines. There were traces of old bush roads that they could follow but which were all but impossible for me, as I recall.

They had a couple of tree stands built of poles, which they called by the Indian name *wigassi*. Arnold was part Indian by blood, the others by nature.

They also had a tiny log shelter at the top of the hill into which one could crawl.

I was a little dubious about hunting with Bert. He had a reputation as a poacher and a pretty rough character. The law and hunting seasons didn't seem to mean much to Bert, and I had often been cautioned about associating with the likes of him. By the end of the next day, however, I had seen a side of him for which I was grateful. It was the type of lesson we all encounter at one time or another—we are jolted into a different perception or humbled by someone for whom we possibly had too little respect. I believe it is called eating crow.

The rain had stopped, and the sky had started to brighten as the moon rose. It was turning colder with frost in the air—conditions that would result in the animals moving about to breed and feed. Arnold was determined to get into a *wigassi* for the opportunity.

As he prepared to leave, Arnold gave instructions. "Be sure to come up first thing in the morning. I expect to have a moose down, and I'll be hungry, so bring me some toast and jam."

The others stayed by the warm fire with us, had a few hot whiskies, and told more than a few stories.

Arnold had barely shut the door when Bert, with a hint of trepidation, suggested we set a net at the falls to catch us some whitefish.

It was a chore I hated. Setting a net in the fast-flowing icy water was an unpleasant ordeal at the best of times. Freezing my hands and being yelled at when the net tangled or the boat tilting didn't appeal to me either although I knew that any take of whitefish was good for the lake. Whitefish are not a game fish. They reduce the number of desirable game fish by eating their young and depleting the food supply. They were overpopulating the lake and were good winter food when salted in a barrel.

Uncle Jim winked at me. "The whitefish aren't running yet," he said.

"Well then, we will get a few pickerel and pike," Bert said.

"Isn't that illegal?" I asked knowingly.

"Wouldn't want to do anything illegal, would you, Bert?" Art remarked. "Let's concentrate on hunting in this trip."

"I hope Arnold made it up the trail. It looks pretty dark out there to me," I commented.

"We're used to traveling in the dark," Art declared. "In fact, for years, I never saw this waterway in the daylight."

Like a kid bragging about stealing cookies, he went on to explain. "We often got our moose out of season. Took them out after dark through Crystal and Miller (lakes). Bert would pick up the meat the next day with a horse and wagon by way of the old bush road into Miller. Then he piled wood on top to hide the moose. Nobody ever caught on."

An awfully difficult trek just to get some moose meat, I thought to myself.

"Do you still do that?" I asked.

"Naw," Bert said. "I'm getting too old. Besides, with the longer moose season, now I get all the hunting I want."

He went outside. "To drain the brine off my pickle," was the expression he used.

I took the opportunity to query Art. "I hear Bert got caught with fresh moose meat in the summer."

"Yea," Art confided, "caught and fined. Judge didn't believe his story that it was an accident."

"An accident?" I asked.

Art explained, "Bert says he heard his cows bawling one night and suspected a bear was after them. So he takes his gun and goes into the pasture in the dark, sees a black object, and shoots it. Turns out to be a moose. Just a damn accident."

"Bad luck," I sympathized.

Bert came back in, shivered, and said, "I need another hot toddy. Any of that cheap whisky left?"

More drinks . . . more stories.

"This whisky doesn't have the kick to it that Alex's had," Bert lamented.

Alex was notorious for his still, and for years, he had outsmarted the Royal Canadian Mounted Police and their reputation for "always getting their man." There were no RCMP in the immediate area, but somehow, they found out about Alex's still and were sent in to gather evidence that would put an end to his operation. But Alex managed to stay one step ahead of them, like the sneaky, crafty wolf he was, and he bragged about it.

He had played in a band and sold his whisky at dances. Hid the whisky in the piano, the story went, and buried his still in the snow or in the bush. He even carved a trail that led the police in the opposite direction. One time, they tramped right over the buried still on their snowshoes. Neighbours would warn Alex when the RCMP was on the way.

One day, they surprised him and caught him with whisky hidden in the water reservoir of his old wood stove. Alex fessed up and, with admiration, said, "You got me this time."

The police were about to take a sample from the reservoir for evidence.

"No need to take from there," Alex said. "I'll get you a bigger bottle from the shed."

Away he went and came back with a big bottle. The police thanked him for his cooperation and left for town.

In the court case that ensued, the bottle was produced as evidence. But Alex countered that he wanted the contents of the bottle tested. Turned out it couldn't be classified as whisky because of a trace of coal oil in the liquid. The case was dismissed.

Then there were also stories about some of those crafty old prospectors (not to mention any names) who salted their claims. (Salting is when high-grade samples from another area are placed in a claim.)

Bert said in a way, he sympathized with "them" hardworking prospectors. All too often, their claims were essentially stolen by rich promoters from Toronto. Certainly, the prospectors were not paid what the claims were worth, according to Bert; and what is good for the goose is good for the gander. Good thing we don't have such a philosophy today. We have too many business scandals, and the polls show upwards of 76 percent of the population think our politicians are dishonest. On second thought, maybe some of our problems in society could be attributed to attitudes such as Bert's.

My uncle commented that it was a shame that for all the millions made in the mines, so little was left for the benefit of the area. He couldn't understand why people, such as Harry Oakes who made millions in the Kirkland Lake mines, were allowed to take their money out of the country to avoid paying Canadian taxes.

"What do you think of the government in this country?" Bert asked me.

But before I can answer, he went on to say with irritation, "We got too much regulation coming out of Toronna and Ottawa from people that don't know their ass from a hole in the ground."

"What makes you say that?" I asked.

"Stupid drinking laws," Bert stated. "Prohibition did more harm than good. Finally got rid of that. Still can't have a whisky in a beverage room. Doesn't make any sense to have separate drinking rooms for men and women." (This law was changed in the late 1960s.)

He went on to describe how, a few years back, a young government inspector had barged into his potato patch, dug up a potato, and said it had a bad disease—some form of blight. He then told Bert to destroy the entire crop. Bert said it didn't look like blight to him, but the lad insisted the crop had to be destroyed. So Bert agreed, but he hid enough potatoes for the winter and for seed in the spring, and his next-year crop was fine. Bert said a man should be compensated by the government for such mistakes. They had no hesitation in fining him when he made one.

Power-hungry politicians and misguided civil servants will ruin this country yet if we let 'em, was Bert's consensus.

Then while playing cribbage, there were more stories.

They talked about Jim Smith, the horse dealer who had fallen on hard times due to the increase of motor vehicles and better roads, now ploughed in the winter. The thought was expressed that he should have taken on a car dealership because they both required a bit of double-dealing. But Jim had stayed with his horse business too long.

The stories turned to the merits of different horses—how each animal has a unique personality and needs to be treated individually to get the best from it, what was or had been the best team in the area, and other stories about people in these parts.

My uncle explained that he could always judge a man by the way he drove a team of horses. Bert claimed that a man has to show an animal who is boss with a firm hand and big stick. For my benefit, my uncle went on to say that the reins had to be held firmly enough to guide the horses but loose enough to allow them to do their job and that there is a time to give them free rein and a time to hold them in check. He further commented that he saw many horses balk when jerked around by the driver. I commented that I saw the similarities to management styles in the large company where I worked.

Although motor vehicles had pretty well ruined Jim Smith's horse dealership by 1950, horses were still the mainstay for timbering operations and on many farms. The delivery business we had sold in 1948 was converted from horse and wagon to motor vehicle by 1949. The Ski-Doo, introduced in 1952, was still an unknown in this area.

Bert talked about the way his sled dogs acted, fought, and pulled.

Looking back, I can't help noticing how we have changed. Today, my generation talks more about cars, electronic gadgets, and sex.

These fellows had a few words of wisdom about women too. You probably know all there is to know on that subject, so I won't repeat here. However, you might find comments about the old trapper's friendly lady an interesting bit of history.

An innocent sounding question was asked, "Have you taken Raymond (the trapper) and his companion up to the shack for the winter yet?"

"No, and I don't plan to," growled Uncle Jim.

"I heard they stay here on the way up in the fall and on the way out in the spring," Bert commented.

"No more," my uncle stated firmly.

"Why's that?" Bert asked with a wink at me. "Heard they smelled pretty bad after a winter in the bush skinning beaver. Can be a foul job."

"The stench was terrible," Uncle confirmed.

"No need for that," Art chipped in. "Could always melt some snow. On the farm, we had no power, running water, or even a bathroom. We did have one of those big round tubs, and Mother gave us a good scrub in the kitchen every Saturday night, whether we needed it or not."

"Same thing with my mother," Bert added. "A habit I still practice."

"Jim, I heard that the trapper's lady wanted to crawl in with you one night. Couldn't blame her after a long winter with that old son of a bitch. Heard you turned the poor thing down," Bert quipped and added, "always respected a man with high morals."

Art and I roared with laughter.

Finally, we all went out in the frosty moonlight to gaze at the stars while taking a final "pickle drain" before climbing into our sleeping bags.

The snoring was immediate and thunderous.

Next morning at the crack of dawn, we were halfway up the trail and met Arnold at the little log shelter.

"There is moose all around us. I heard them all night," he whispered as he gulped down toast and hot coffee from a thermos.

He had a strategy for the experienced old bushmen and me.

As we set out to take our positions, Arnold cautioned me, "Stay on the trail or in the *wigassi*. It's easy to get lost in here, and we won't have time to find you." I guess Arnold thought I looked pretty wet behind the ears.

I felt a little put down by this, but my mind soon wandered down another path. This type of hunting, in such a big unknown area, was new to me; and after five years in the city, I could feel that I was already losing some of my sense of direction. In the past, I instinctively had known north from south, like a native or a goose, and never had to resort to a compass. I didn't have one now. I sometimes wonder how many of our antennae and senses have been dulled by our urban lifestyle.

Clouds had rolled in. I wasn't sure which way to head if I did get lost. Which way was west? I hadn't been observant enough of the twists and turns along the way, and I had simply followed the leader. Perhaps that is an apt metaphor for life. If you don't pay attention, you run the risk of getting lost or being led down the garden path.

That morning, we saw one moose, but he outsmarted us though we did get two deer.

I wondered about this then and still wonder from time to time. How come the deer and moose were in the same feed area? Deer carry a tick that kills moose. They aren't supposed to be able to live together, yet for a number of years, the moose and deer had cohabited in this area. Eventually, the deer disappeared completely.

With all our knowledge, one would think we would be capable of controlling wildlife numbers. It is true. As I document earlier, we have had some outstanding successes overall. However, there are still pockets of fluctuations and devastating losses in wildlife. For example, Algonquin Park (a huge park, 7,725 square kilometres) was well known for the numerous deer that were protected and that could be approached and fed by hand. This was a feature that helped attract millions of visitors interested in wildlife. Unfortunately, deer have almost vanished in the past few years along with other wildlife. The weather, food supply, and habitat conditions caused by man are significant factors. Mother Nature also seems to play a role that we don't fully understand. We still can learn and do much to improve management of wildlife, in my opinion.

Personally, I am anxiously waiting for science to provide me with the immune system of a fish, the digestive system of an owl, the gracefulness of a deer, the strength of a bear, and the sex life of a—I haven't finished my list yet. I guess hunters are always searching for something.

We cut up our deer and loaded the meat into a couple of packsacks weighing seventy to eighty pounds each. It was a long carryout, and to save a tough mile walk, Arnold kept an canvas-covered, leaky old canoe on a lake created by beavers at the top of the hill. Freeze-up was expected soon, so the old canoe was to be taken out. The others headed down the trail.

"I'll take the packsack," Bert announced.

That left the canoe for me. My heart sank. I knew I could not carry that heavy water-logged load down the steep, slippery hill. It was already dusk. I was dog-tired and concerned that I might injure myself but was too proud to admit such weakness.

Bert must have seen the look on my face. "I'll take the canoe too," he said. "You have a long drive ahead of you back to Montreal. Just help me set it on top of the pack to protect my shoulders."

Away he went carrying a load of over two hundred pounds with a tumpline pressed to his forehead. He didn't stop until we reached the lake, three-quarters of a mile below.

I could hardly believe the strength and stamina of this man who was in his sixties at the time. At the time, he seemed almost ancient to me.

I was very indebted for his act of consideration and couldn't help but admire the old rascal. I was surprised at his sensitivity and the way he let me save face. Under that rough, tough exterior was a heart of gold. Eating crow doesn't often come with such a grateful feeling. Well, that is not quite right. Situations that occur in the wilderness often make one sigh with relief and eat a bit of crow.

What drives men to hunt and endure the torture? It has to be an animal spirit or instinct that is not logical to a nonhunter.

Another story with more points to ponder

Some find this story interesting, some funny, and some cruel or a bit barbaric. For me, it was an exciting learning experience, one connected directly to our hunter-gatherer heritage that dates back to man's beginnings. We like to be with friends, to be close to nature and her creatures, and to enjoy a challenge.

For our moose hunt this particular year, we had decided to tent on Moose Lake so that from our canoe, hopefully, we could call a moose out to the shore for an easy shot and carry. Well, it wouldn't really be an easy carry considering the three portages still to cross on our way home, just easier than the experience of the past few years. My brother-in-law made a little stove so we would be warm and cosy in the tent for a change. We would even be able to dry our cold, wet clothes.

In case there were no moose close to the lake, we chose a location to camp where we could walk to the Big Valley through the Little Notch. We knew there were lots of moose there. I drove the six hundred kilometres north Friday after work, and it took us most of Saturday to transport our provisions by canoe and over the portages to our destination.

It was a cold, drizzly day. The portages on the way up the Wendigo chain of lakes were wet and slippery, and my partners left the heaviest packs for me, or so it seemed. I slipped once or twice under those heavy loads.

"You would be wise not to carry so much and make an extra trip. You could hurt yourself and ruin our hunt," I was advised by my caring buddies.

In the late afternoon, it started to clear up; and as we were setting up camp, a small plane landed across the lake and dropped off a couple of hunters. *Damn it*, I thought, *All they will do is scare the moose back from the lake*. Sometimes, we disliked hunters.

That evening, after we called for moose without any luck from our canoe, the other hunters dropped in with a couple of beers to say hello. They were from Toronto and wanted to know how we got there. The outfitter that flew them in had told them this was a remote lake, with access only by plane. They wanted to know if they could hunt with us since we appeared to know what we were doing.

"You're welcome to join us," I said. "Tomorrow, we're taking the moose trail that goes up through the Little Notch and over the hill in back of us into a big valley. It's a tough half-mile climb up and then down the other side, but that's where most of the moose are. You'll need a good big packsack to carry out the meat."

They opted to take their chances on the lake and left.

They looked at us as if we were crazy. Well, maybe we were. It has been said that you don't have to be crazy to hunt, but it helps. After reading the following little episode, you may put your own connotation on "crazy." It can be interpreted as "different," "daring," "adventuresome," "bizarre," or "berserk."

Early the next morning when I woke up, it was still dark; and during the night, it had turned bitterly cold.

I put my hand to my nose. It felt like an icicle—a dripping icicle. I needed to pee in the worst way but hated to leave the warmth of the sleeping bag. I lay in discomfort for a while then finally forced myself to jump up, pull on some heavy socks over my long johns, and dance out the tent on frost-covered ground. I shivered in the cold, gave a moose call, and listened for an answer.

I had mixed feelings. A heavy fog had drifted in from the lake. If there was a moose close by, he might charge. Should I really be challenging a 1,200-pound adversary under these conditions?—and in my underwear at that!

I crawled back into the tent and lit the little stove. The others were huddled in their sleeping bags like turtles in shells, except turtles don't sleep with toques on their heads. I rubbed my hands, absorbing the joy of heat from the crackling fire. I broke the ice in the pail of water and put on a pot of coffee then cooked some bacon. I searched for the eggs and finally found them outside in one of the packs. I tapped one on the edge of the fry pan. It didn't crack. I thought, *The chickens in the north must be hardy to make such tough shells*, and I banged the egg harder on the pan. The damn thing bounced like an Indian rubber ball.

"Maybe they are frozen," some wise guy mumbled from the warmth of his bag. "Set them in some warm water. We'll keep them in the tent tonight."

"Do you think that will help?" the muffled voice of the other turtle quipped.

It shouldn't be so cold in October.

We ate quickly and set off over the mountain with our big packsacks, hunting knives, rope, hatchets, maps, compasses, signal whistles, guns, and ammo. We were ready for the moose and lady luck. I was convinced that this was my year for a moose.

After three-quarters of an hour of huffing and puffing up the hill and through the swamp, "I'm headed for the bullring on the far side of the beaver pond," I said. It was a spot where there were always good signs.

We separated, the other two going wherever their instincts, or moose trails, took them.

By ten thirty, the sun was getting warm, and I weary. I had been walking for over three hours, so I decided to sit close to a moose trail and to wait for a curious moose that might search out the intruder. I dozed off.

I was wakened suddenly by a gunshot. I recognized the sound as coming from Bob's .30-30. I said to myself, *That lucky beggar.* I took a compass bearing for direction and listened for the normal second insurance shot. None came. *He must have missed*, I reckoned. Maybe the scared moose would run down this trail towards me. I sneaked quietly towards the shot.

All of a sudden, I heard the blast of a whistle, then another, and another in quick succession! It was a distress signal—something was wrong! I started to run and soon burst into a little clearing by a beaver dam. There on top of a knoll sat Bob, his rifle pointed at a huge bull moose whose large antlers were rotating back and forth, like a radar antenna.

"He's stuck in the gully, and if he dies there, we'll never get him out!" Bob shouted.

The animal, paralyzed by the bullet that hit him on the backbone hump, had dropped into a little gully and clay ditch that had been formed by flowing water in the spring runoff. He was wedged there as if in a vice. How to get him out was the question. We knew that if he died there, his meat would be wasted.

"If I get him mad enough at me," I said, "he'll come up out of there and charge me. You keep your gun pointed at him, and as soon as he jumps up, shoot him real quick!"

I sneaked, matador fashion, head-on towards him with my rifle held across in front of me like a fighting staff. He rotated his big sixty-inch rack while looking wild-eyed at me, but he didn't budge otherwise. A fallen tree across the little gully, between the moose and me, offered some protection.

"I'm going to get close enough to hit his horns with the butt of my gun. That will bring him to life," I announced bravely.

I inched closer, and as he rotated his rack in my direction, I met it with the butt of my rifle with a loud smack! He leapt up but fell right back in the hole.

By this time, the third member of our party had arrived to find out what all the commotion was about. He was a lanky lad dressed in baggy old pants with shirttail loosely hanging and feet planted in a pair of oversized knee-high rubber boots. He looked more like Ichabod Crane than a hunter.

I instructed him, "Get a stick, and when he jumps up, hit him on the rump—that should get him moving."

I sneaked towards the moose again with all the confidence and caution of a bullfighter and smacked his horns with the butt of my gun once more. He leapt in the air, my buddy whacked him on his rump, and the moose came around the fallen tree at me. But he dropped into the ditch again.

Now I didn't have the protection of the tree, but we still had to get the moose out of the ditch.

We knew he had lost much of his strength, but how much strength he was regaining was also on our minds.

We decided to repeat the procedure with much caution. When I hit his horn—this time, he jumped up—the lad thumped his rump with a stick, and the moose charged. As I ran, my brother-in-law fired several shots. Glancing over my shoulder, I was surprised to see Ichabod running behind me with flailing arms and shirttail flying. Right on his tail was the charging bull, head lowered, ready to pitchfork him. How my buddy got into this predicament is still a mystery to me. He must have panicked and ran in the wrong direction. As I veered behind a tree, I turned and fired my .30-06 and hit the moose in the chest. He dropped dead a few feet from me as Ichabod, in his rubber boots, went by at surprising speed!

As we were dressing the moose, I observed only two wounds—one from Bob's first shot in addition to mine, so I asked, "What were you shooting at when he came after me?"

"I was shooting at his head," he replied. "I wanted to tuck one right behind his ear so we wouldn't waste any meat."

I grumbled something about that being a low-percentage shot. For him, to risk my life for a couple of pounds of moose meat didn't thrill me. I also had a few words of wisdom for the guy in the rubber boots.

We had a close look at the head and found a couple of leads lodged just under the skin. The bullets hadn't even cracked the hard skull. We cut up the 1,400-pound moose and took it and his horns out in packsacks and went about two miles up the four-hundred-foot-high steep climb and down again, across six lakes in a canoe, plus three portages and some rapids. It took us four days of hard, heavy work to carry him out and another day of meat cutting to prepare him for the table. His meat was especially tender and delicious.

His horns still hang over the fireplace in the cottage—a real conversation piece. When I tell the story, I am never sure whether the audience is laughing with me or at me. But then, as the Spanish proverb says, "It is not the same to talk of bulls as to be in the bullring."

Horns over fireplace.

Occasionally, I see a turned-up nose and receive a barb about the cruelty of tormenting and killing the animal.

In fact, I have tussled with the issue myself and have reached the following perspective that I hope has meaning for you.

The hunt and kill is an event in nature that I have witnessed hundreds of times, and each time, it causes some uneasiness in me that on reflection turns to awe or wonderment at how nature functions. For example, I recently watched a wildlife film showing a pack of wolves stalking and bothering a herd of caribou for days before managing to separate one from the herd. They then attacked viciously, and the poor animal retreated into the icy river. The wolves waited; and when, hours later, the victim struggled back to shore in a weakened state, they finished the kill. I have left out much detail because, for many people, it is a very disturbing scene. So is a cat-and-mouse scene where the cat plays and torments the mouse until it perishes. Even watching a horde of ants attacking a caterpillar is disquieting for me until I put it into perspective as one of the many and mysterious ways in which the world works.

I have decided that in order to maintain my sanity, I can either ignore the perceived pain in the realities of the cycle of life or accept the fact that there are some things I might never understand. I have chosen the latter and feel a reverence for our Creator and his system. I believe that, somehow, the hunted are compensated in a way not obvious to us in terms of nervous system and pain relief. It seems reasonable to me to assume that animal spirits go somewhere, based on a scientific maxim that energy is never lost but simply changes form. Perhaps their spirits go to some useful place—who knows where? I remind myself that man is part of nature, part of the equation. What happens is part of life, and without death, there is no life. I ask myself, How dare we deny the divinity of an immortal creature and the cycle of life that includes birth, death, the possibility of rebirth, and everything in between?

Native hunters usually felt a kind of animal divinity whereby the animal gives its life with the understanding that it transcends its physical entity. The hunter thanked the animal for the food. In this case, the moose dropped, paralyzed by the bullet. While I was challenging him, I did not sense he was in great pain. I detected something in his glaring eyes that was probably defiance as he rotated his horns at me in the same fashion he would had I been another bull. He reacted to a whack on his bum, one that was not a brutal attack—anyone who has dealt with a mischievous horse or cow will understand what I am saying.

This moose's ordeal lasted less than an hour. Compare this to a fate of most moose at the hands of a wolf, a bear, starvation, disease, or being hit and mangled by a train or motor vehicle. The movie *March of the Penguins* is an excellent documentary that illustrates the nature of things. In this movie, there are heartwarming moments and heartrendering moments. The fact is that nature appears to be crueller than man.

That aside, I continue to encourage all hunters to make the kill as clean as possible. More often than not, one or two quick shots should do the job.

Perhaps the real pain was inflicted on us. We had to gut him, cut him into packsack-sized chunks that we could barely carry, and transport him up the mountain and down the treacherous steep cliff on the other side. Just thinking about it triggers the pain all over again in my shoulders, back, and legs.

The above incident causes me to ponder the native belief that the animal delivers itself to you, and I see signs that support this notion. Consider the following: It was a beautiful warm autumn day with no wind, sounds, or other distractions. A moose can hear or smell a human a mile away. We weren't using any camouflage scent or clothes. In fact, my brother-in-law had removed a rubber boot because his sweaty sock or a piece of dirt was causing him discomfort. While standing there balancing on one foot with the other airing, he happened to look up and saw this big moose about one hundred feet away walking towards him silently on a little trail in heavy bush. Bob slowly reached for his rifle, and as he gently raised it and cocked the hammer, the moose turned enough for any easy shot into his vulnerable hump.

Whether or not the animal delivers himself, or it is just plain luck, we will never know. I suggest that hunting is similar to the rest of life. Luck comes most often to those who are well prepared.

I know that the foregoing experience impacted me tremendously. For months, my spirits were exalted. The emotions are tough to describe. I can definitely identify with a lady who explained how she felt after bagging her first moose. She said the only other experience that came close to it was giving birth to her first child. Many others express similar feelings.

For me, the Spanish philosopher Ortega y Gasset made an observation worth considering when he said, "If we want to enjoy that intense and pure happiness which is a 'return to nature,' we have to seek the company of the surly beast, descend to his level, feel emulation toward him, pursue him, and this subtle rite is the hunt."

Ortega went on to say that nonhunters will wince because they are certain that the biking trip or backpacking outing they've known is return to nature enough. But the true hunters will know that Ortega is right.

The chase

This story demonstrates that many friends do not necessarily enjoy the same kind of hunting but nonetheless can have a hunting experience together that is remembered fondly.

Some Toronto friends of mine asked if I would take them moose hunting. Their hunting experience had been limited to small game and birds. So late in the fall, four of us headed north. I showed them topographical maps of the area and explained that we were going into difficult terrain where it was easy to get lost. Compasses were checked to familiarize them with the direction of the waterway and so on. When I detected some uneasiness, I pointed out trails and places where they would be safe, explaining that I would head out to find where the moose were and perhaps, in the process, would flush one out to them.

We packed lunches and set out early the following morning.

I wandered into close-by beaver ponds, but there were no fresh signs. I kept heading northeast, knowing I would eventually run into moose or at least good fresh signs. After several hours, I was getting discouraged. I had travelled so far back into the bush that I wondered about our ability to carry out the meat if I did shoot one. I sat on a fallen tree and quietly ate lunch. A squirrel kept chattering from a clump of spruce and balsam trees.

It had started to snow, and it was time for me to head out, but I decided to take one last look in the clump of trees where a squirrel had been chattering. I saw fresh moose tracks, stopped, and listened.

All of a sudden, there was a tremendous commotion with moose running in several directions, almost trampling me! I was so startled, and they were so quick that I didn't get a shot away. As things settled down, I realized that I had stumbled into the middle of a sleeping family of four moose who had panicked and jumped into action.

That night, I explained what had happened to the others and suggested that since I had not fired a shot or chased them, the moose had probably stayed in the area. With the aid of the snow, we could probably get one. My friends said that as long as I assured them that they wouldn't get lost, they were prepared for the hard work of carrying packsacks loaded with cut-up moose meat. One guy said, "Not me. I'll stay on a trail close to the camp."

Next morning, three of us started to follow my tracks in the snow. After two hours of walking, we came to the previous day's moose beds. My companions were to spread out on the snow trail, and I started to follow the moose tracks, hoping to get a moose or to drive one towards them. The tracks led me in an almost straight line west to a rock cliff that dropped straight down three hundred feet. The moose had walked along the edge until they came to a little notch where they literally slid down the rock face. *These moose are more like mountain goats*, I thought to myself and slid down too. I found where they had crossed at the top of the falls on their way to the other side of the lake. So I returned to my friends who were shivering in the cold.

We built a small fire, sat, and ate lunch. I told the group about my morning and that I had crossed another fresh track not far away, probably made by a single young bull. I wanted to try tracking him.

It had started to snow again. My friends said they were afraid that the snow would cover our tracks, and without them or me, they would not be able to find their way out.

We agreed they should head out right away and make their way back to the boat before the tracks became covered. I suggested they watch the lake from the cottage because a moose might cross there, or I might chase the young bull out that way. I advised them that it would take me about four hours to reach the lake and for them to be on the lookout for me. I didn't know exactly where I might come out. I would be very tired and therefore would certainly appreciate being picked up by boat.

Off they went at a near gallop, and I started to track my bull. He was headed south and kept going in that direction. A couple of times, I heard him when he cracked a branch, but the wily rascal kept out of sight. Finally, he must have become nervous and took off. I kept following the tracks because, according to my compass, he was headed in the direction where my buddies might get a shot at him.

Finally, I came out at a little point just south and east of the cottage where I noted the moose had entered the water to swim across the lake to lose me. I couldn't understand why my buddies had not fired a shot. Had they not been watching? The snow had turned to a freezing drizzle. I looked across the bay and could see smoke billowing out the fireplace chimney. The front window was completely fogged up. I couldn't get anybody's attention, even by firing a couple of shots into the air; so I set out on the tough walk to reach the cottage, which I finally reached, dog-tired. I opened the door and walked in. They were startled and a bit embarrassed to see me as they sat warming themselves by the fire, drinking hot rum.

"Didn't you see that moose!" I exclaimed.

"What moose?" Jack asked nonchalantly.

"The one I've been chasing since morning," I said in a not-too-friendly tone. I pointed across the bay and declared, "He came out at that point and crossed the lake less than one hundred yards away."

Bill excitedly jumped up, grabbed his coat and gun, and said, "I want you to take me and show me that track."

I felt like handing him a basket and telling him to go gather the tracks because that was all he was going to get for supper. But I was too played out, so I said in a meek manner, "I sure would appreciate if someone could pour me a drink while I get out of these wet clothes." I was soaked to the skin from the snow and freezing rain. They started hustling to pour me a hot drink and to warm up some stew.

We remained great friends, but they informed me that they did not like certain aspects of my kind of moose hunt. Bill wrote this poem s few years later and presented it at a surprise party they held on my fiftieth birthday.

THE CHASE by Bill Towers

A late Fall trip to Englehart, when the weather is bleak and cold,
With a gun and canoe, and a bottle or two, this sport is for none
but the bold.
To live in a tent, where the elements are bent, to test the best
of men,
To Ralph it's a challenge he can't resist, for he's been back again
and again.

*He awakes before dawn, packs a lunch and he's gone, for the
    hunt has now begun.*
*To come back at dusk, when return he must, with the look of a
    man having fun.*
*He relates over stew, by the camp fire's hue, of the moose he had
    chased that day*
*From an old logging trail, across hill and dale, to a swamp about
    10 miles away.*

*He begins the next day, much the same way, but this time he
    starts in the swamp.*
*He picks up the trail, of the moose he had tailed, and nothing
    his spirits would damp.*
*And he chased that moose 10 miles or more, back where he had
    started the day before.*

*As the days went by, and they seemed to fly, Ralph had yet to
    fire his gun.*
*But pack he must, and by God he cussed, for the freeze-up had
    begun.*
*So with a face that's grim, not at all like him, he has to get out
    of here.*
*For it would be foolish to stay, just one more day, so late in the
    Fall of the year.*
Now it's back to Joan, the boys and his home, back to life in the city.
*But he will return to be sure, to chase the son of a whore, to be
    denied would be a pity.*

*Now as the years take hold, and Ralph gets old, and can no
    longer take part in the chase,*
*On a hill he can stand, while surveying the land, and remembering
    the good old days.*

*   *   *

The unfolding of a hunt portrayed by photos

During the hunt, there is beauty, hardship, adventure, happiness, sadness, gratitude, and, of course, death—similar to life itself. In fact, hunting can be viewed as a metaphor or a snapshot of life. Early natives used hunting in a ritual to initiate youths into adulthood in which they learned responsibility, self-worth, teamwork, and respect for all life.

Due to the many problems in our society today, perhaps the time is ripe to reintroduce hunting as a rite of passage. This book is intended to guide us towards that path.

The trip to get there.

The falls portage.

This is our version of a wigassi (Indian word for "tree stand" where a hunter watches, waits, and tries to entice his prey by imitating the mating call).

Views while watching and listening day after day for the elusive moose.

Warming up after sitting for a long period in the cold.

*Cooling down after a long walk in
heavy bush looking for moose.*

*Enjoying an interlude between morning and
evening hunt by fishing.*

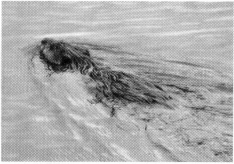

View from the cottage deck whilewatching for moose or any
sights and sounds of wildlife such as beaver,fish jumping,
cry of a wolf, hoot of an owl, whispering pines,
or just enjoying the evening quietly.

This shows my son Richard and his payoff
after several years of no luck.

Two moose came out to him. An experience like this often brings forth a strange mixture of feelings—immense excitement, satisfaction, and awe. It left Richard a bit shaken and sad due to the demise of such beautiful animals, but then great joy overcame him, and we see him holding the head as a trophy. Later, he talked about his surprise and pounding heart when he looked up and saw the moose standing less than fifty yards away. He quickly shot one of them but didn't have the heart to shoot the other and let it walk away, disappearing into the bush. However, when it reappeared, he thought it was meant to be, so he fired another shot. Both moose succumbed immediately after one shot each—a bit unusual for an animal the size of a moose.

Hauling one of the moose out of a beaver pond.

Field dressing a moose is a messy job. For some, the task causes a bit of queasiness. Others take pride in their surgical skill that is fundamental in the process of preparing food. Overall, this team was thrilled with the experience. It sparked excitement and reactions similar to what occurs when one scores a goal or the team wins. This emotional childlike outburst possibly harks back to our roots when we were hunter-gatherers, and capturing a large food supply inspired a hurrah and celebration.

Backpacking at the lake with eighty-five pounds of cut-up moose.

Loading the canoe with moose meat.

Arriving at camp with a canoe load of moose meat.

*Lifting heavy pieces of moose to hang for cleaning and aging
in readiness for a meat cutter.*

*Hung moose and a nice trout caught by
Eli while patrolling the lake.*

Taking a rest while enjoying a little libation.

Taking a much-needed bath in ice-cold water.

Coats hanging to dry on moose horns.

*A toast with special thanks for our luck and for a delicious
meal of nutritious moose stew.*

*With a full belly, animals rest. This is what we are doing while
enjoying some music.*

Leaving to go back to life in the city.

CHAPTER 7

Bear stories

Stories about bear experiences are also told and retold at most hunt camps. Many people avoid wilderness experiences because of their fear of bears. Surveys have shown that the majority, even those who enjoy camping, prefer the organized sites where other people are nearby. I suppose it is partly due to the increased news coverage of bear incidents combined with the fear of the unknown. I hope these stories of my encounters with bears help to put the risk and fears in perspective. It is a shame not to experience the wilderness.

Wilderness animals usually prefer to stay out of sight. On most occasions when a human encounters one, they get out of the way if given a chance. Black bears are not nearly as aggressive as grizzly bears. Attacks, which occur very infrequently, usually occur in areas where man has allowed wild animals to get used to his presence, such as in parks and around garbage dumps. Even there, the risk is extremely low. Researchers Stephen Herrero and Lynn Rogers make the point that black bears are actually quite tolerant of humans and that in national parks, there are thousands of incidents without even minor injuries occurring. Very occasionally, there is a rogue animal.

Rogue humans are much more common and dangerous. The fact is that the risk is much greater in everyday life in our cities.

Bears are smart creatures but can be extremely vicious and destructive. They have voracious appetites, and male bears will fight mother bears and devour her cubs. A bear will eat everything contained in a human's diet and more—including insects, roots, berries, bird's eggs, and a host of other animals (mice, fox, beaver, for example). I have already stated that they kill 30 to70 percent of moose and elk calves annually, depending on the region. Literature on what to do when you meet a bear is available at local wildlife services, in books, and on the Internet. It goes without saying that humans encountering bears in the wild should approach them with respect, poise, and always in a nonthreatening manner. The same can be said when approaching all animals, especially large animals or those likely to retaliate—which includes humans, I suppose.

Several times I have been within a few feet of a bear that could easily have had me for dinner. I have stumbled onto them at the cottage and in the bush while quietly hunting or fishing.

Bear story one

Just before dawn one summer morning, one greeted me face-to-face at the cottage. He was standing tall, his front paws against the screen door looking into the kitchen and sniffing. I was undressed with my paws ready to push the door open on my way out to the privy. He was as startled as I was and backed up quickly but didn't run away. I woke my wife and mother so they could see him, and I allowed him to linger around and watched him eating blueberries. He returned to look at me through the screen of an open kitchen window. At the click of my camera, he charged up a tree. *Geez, if he jumps on this old roof, his weight might carry him through. Then what will I do?* I asked myself.

Luckily, he backed down the tree and wandered over for one last sniff and last look at me before finally ambling off. It was exciting entertainment for me though it made my wife and mother a little nervous as they peered out the window.

Bear running away.

Bear story two

A few years ago, I came across a den while hunting. I wondered what kind of animal it harboured. The "doorway" appeared too small for a bear and so was the mound of earth around the entrance. I also reckoned it was a bit too early for bears to be hibernating. It wasn't at all like a wolf's den. A big raccoon perhaps? They normally did not live this far north, but with global warming, they had started to appear in nearby towns. There being no visible tracks, my curiosity got the better of me, so down I went on hands and knees to peer into the den. In the dark hole, I saw what looked like a little paw move! I jumped back, and immediately, a two-hundred-to-three-hundred-pound black bear exploded out the opening! He made a quick turn to avoid me and disappeared into the thick underbrush! I couldn't believe an animal that big could squeeze out that little opening, and so quickly. The little paw I had seen must have been a big toe. Prior to this incident, I had always assumed that the law about bothering bears in their dens had been written to protect the bears!

Bear story three

One time while fishing quietly, we anchored our canoe near shore at a rapids and looked up to see four cubs tumbling playfully over the boulders towards us. They stopped a few yards from the canoe peering curiously and sniffing at us. We sat, silently watching. I was a little nervous because we were so close to shore. Mother bear was sure to show up and could easily jump us and upset the canoe. All of a sudden, the mother bear did appear and screamed at her cubs who took off at a gallop, their mother chasing them. We could hear her scolding them until the five of them were out of hearing range.

Bear story four

On another occasion, my three young sons who had been playing outside the cottage came running in to excitedly announce that there was a wounded baby bear outside. I sauntered out, only half believing their imaginative spirits. But sure enough, a small bear with a deformed front paw, weighing about one hundred pounds—about the size of a big bulldog—was exploring his and our surroundings. He got into the garbage and hung around for a while before ambling off. My mother and my wife were adamant that, henceforth, all the garbage be burned immediately. I rather enjoyed the visiting beast and took the occasion to talk to the boys about the need to be cautious, but not fearful, and to speak firmly so the bear would not be surprised or threatened by their presence.

Bear story five

One spring day when snow was still on the ground, my cousin spotted a huge bear high up at the top of a large poplar tree. This was unusual because it was early for bears to be out of hibernation and to be so high in a tree. The bear reached out with a manlike arm, grabbed the end of a branch with his paw, pulled the branch in, and ate the buds at the very tip. We wondered why this bear was going to all that trouble; but bears had been acting strangely and boldly that year—walking into farmer's yards, killing dogs, and harassing farm animals. My aunt had an explanation—the fresh buds of the poplar tree were used in early native medicine as a cure for headache, and the bear probably had some form of rabies that causes a headache. He was just using a natural remedy to cure his headache. Are they really that smart? I think so. They have been observed healing themselves in other naturopathic ways.

Bear story six

We are warned that mother bears are particularly dangerous if they feel their cubs are at risk. This is true, but even in such circumstances, they will usually find a way out rather than attack a human. There have been many incidents around farms where cubs have been shot with the mother growling but staying out of sight.

Here is one of my experiences that supports my claim that the dangers about bears are often exaggerated. My brother-in-law doesn't like me telling this story because he feels he acted a little irrationally, but this is not so. When we are caught by surprise, we all react—sometimes in unpredictable, strange ways. We were fishing in a remote area and had stored our catch in a cool cave to preserve it until we were ready to go home. We had been staying in a small log shack, and when it was time to leave, Bob took two large tin minnow pails to get the fish. I stayed by the lake packing up the canoe. For some reason, I looked up and saw Bob frozen in his tracks with his arms outstretched wide apart, each hand holding a bucket of fish. He looked back and forth, east and west, with a wide-eyed expression of surprise on his face. To the west of him, the baby bears were in the doorway of the shack! To the east stood mother bear staring at Bob, her head slightly tilted in the air sniffing at him and his fish. What was she about to do? Was she more interested in the fish or in Bob or in protecting her cubs? Bob wasn't about to spend time wondering; and after a couple of quick glances at the mother on one side of him and the cubs on the other, in panic, he tossed the buckets of fish in the air and came running full tilt towards the canoe. As the metal pails clanged on the rocks, the mother bear hissed loudly and took off in the opposite direction, her cubs galloping after her as fast as they could. I began to laugh, and Bob did too. We took our fish home but left the fish innards for the bears.

Sometimes, I tell the above story to friends in an attempt to quell their anxiety over bears, but it occasionally backfires, and they make snide comments about my sanity. I have a chuckle anyway.

CHAPTER 8

More stories and psychological implications

Psychology is a complex topic. Library shelves are filled with books on psychology. There are numerous interactive factors that affect human behaviour; and many of them are not obvious, easy to grasp, or even understood. To gain an appreciation of these complexities is usually hard work and can be frustrating, especially in a society that is anxious for one-page explanations, scientific proof, and fast fixes. So I am fully aware there may be criticism that my approach here is oversimplified. Nonetheless, I hope that the following short dissertation is meaningful.

Often, insights come to us in strange ways. In his book *The Bear-Walker*, Basil H. Johnston relates a beautiful old Indian story that illustrates this for me in such an interesting way that I want to share it with you. Perhaps it will encourage you to bear with me in my discussions of behavioural considerations relative to hunting. Here is my paraphrased version

> In a parable called "The Bear-Walker," a young man wanted to learn all kinds of things, including understanding himself and how to help his fellow man. He went to many places seeking answers. Eventually, he was referred to a wise old medicine man. This man, sometimes called a Bear-Walker, agreed to try to teach the young man in finding whatever he was looking for. But he was cautioned that it would not be a fast process.
>
> They went walking and stopped to gaze into a river. The young man was asked if he saw anything. Nothing was the reply. So they kept walking and stopping now and then with the same question receiving the same reply.

That evening, the student complained that he was not being taught anything. "You didn't see yourself in the water," the teacher commented.

Early next morning, they went walking again and stopped by a stagnant pond that had many beautiful water lilies. The Bear-Walker asked the young man to get him a particular flower.

The student went in the water up to his knees but was told the desired flower was farther out. The procedure was repeated several times; and the desired flower was not reached until the student was up to his neck in the murky, stagnant, stinking water.

The young man was about to break off the stem when he was told not to break the stem and to retrieve the entire plant. But pull as hard as he could, the plant would not give way. He asked what he could do.

"You're the one out there. Think what you should do," the teacher answered.

After pulling some more, the young man finally dove and dug in the stinking water to get the entire plant, roots and all. He now stank himself.

He was asked to think about what he had learned. Only that the old man really wanted the plant was the reply.

Rather than carry on, the student quit because of the slowness of the teaching.

He went back to the city, and much later during the winter while sitting, the young man suddenly exclaimed, "That's it! That's what he tried to teach me! If you want to help your fellow human beings generally—however you may hate it, however unpleasant it may be—you must work at it. Although everything on the surface of the water may be beautiful, to get to the source of true beauty, you must dig deep." This process is not always beautiful.

*   *   *

In spite of all the denunciation of hunting, the instinct to hunt is so strong in some boys that they initiate themselves into hunting. They go into fields or wooded areas where they search for frogs, birds, and other small animals. They experiment with stalking and pursuing while playing cowboys and Indians and cops and robbers with make-believe weapons as well as with some real ones, such as bows and arrows, blowguns, and slingshots. In the small-town, rural setting where I grew up, I was keen in pursuing these activities starting at a very early age. However, many parents feel hunting is deplorable and discourage or forbid participation in it.

After I moved to the city, my longing lingered for the hunting terrain with its beautiful lakes; rugged hills; stately pine, spruce, and birch; the smell of the bush; sights and sounds; the animal tracks; the solitude; and the chance to unwind. All this kept me returning to the place if just for a weekend to harvest a few partridge on Thanksgiving weekend. For me, there is no other Thanksgiving like it.

Celebrating Thanksgiving with my boys and their cousins.

My wife always encouraged me even when we had three small children and a limited budget. She had a feel for the physical and psychological benefits for me and indirectly to her. We also spent our summer vacations there even though, for her, there was much hardship due to the lack of modern amenities—for example, no power, indoor plumbing, diaper service, or road access.

In this remote setting, there were new experiences for the children— diving from a high rock cliff, the frogs, the fish, and the bonfires with roasted marshmallows. All the little creatures that showed up to scold, look for food, or investigate caused a smile. The sights and sounds of the night—the howl of the wolf, the hoot of the owl, the call of a loon, the slap of a beaver tail on the water, and the colourful northern lights in a star-studded sky—make one linger and listen in the moonlight. Occasionally, the bloodcurdling sound of a screeching, snarling struggle between creatures is heard—one fighting to take a life, one to keep it.

Wood carvings by Bob Beach (now deceased)—brother-in-law, hunting and fishing buddy, and naturalist.

Painting of a beaver.

Hawk eating what seems to be a partridge.

Pet squirrel

Here is a poem my son Tim wrote for a school project when he was 13.

Progress

Have you ever had the simple pleasure of seeing the sun at its rising?
Have you ever been canoeing on a lake just as the fog's arriving?
How about a squirrel in a tree, nibbling on a nut?
Or the smell of a pine tree just after the trunk's been cut?

Have you ever seen the sunrise over all the pollution?
There's no time to go canoeing in our lake of chemical solutions.
How about a mashed up squirrel, smashed by a Plymouth Fury?
You can't smell the pine tree any more. We chopped them down in our hurry.

Hurry to do what you say? Why to make progress my friend,
To make factories, houses and highways, why there is no end
To what we can do if we work really hard and try.
We've made man-made lakes, artificial snow and buildings 80 stories high.

We haven't made progress, we've only destroyed the beauty we knew before.
God put us on this earth to love and not to make war.
This world has not totally cooled and yet it's coming to an end.
Have we done a good or bad job? Think about it my friend.

-Tim Gibbins-

*   *   *

For a hunting spirit to survive in the city requires both a craving and much motivation. It is easy to lose it to other pursuits. To go hunting, one has to be keen to pay the price of conforming to all the hunting and gun regulations, overcome family needs, and travel for miles from our cities to a suitable place.

I gave up hunting large animals for several years, partly because of business priorities and partly because of the stigma attached to hunting in my urban world. Many people are swayed by the shame attached to hunting as promoted by various vocal and powerful antihunting forces, conservation extremists, and antigun groups who are present in our schools, the media, and governments. Debunking hunting seems to be a mission for some who appear to have an almost-psychological need to find fault in the activity. And then there is Walt Disney and *Bambi* to contend with. I have had mixed feelings about taking the life of an animal for what can appear to be an unnecessary reason. I also have concerns about the approach of some hunters to hunting.

As already pointed out, I have come to grasp more fully the paradoxes in life, of which hunting is one, and to appreciate that there is a positive side to hunting when done with consideration and in the right spirit. All activities in life benefit from such an attitude. I hope you will agree.

*   *   *

Although I had given up hunting large animals for reasons explained above, when I retired, my middle son persuaded me to go moose hunting with him and his friends who had not been having any luck.

My return to the rugged terrain of my old hunting haunts rekindled many memories. The form of hunting is a tad unusual as indicated in previously related stories. My savvy in the hunting grounds, the physical exertion, the fresh air, the overall exposure to nature, and the camaraderie were exhilarating as were our successes and the delicious food this provided.

I love the challenge of stalking the animals and trying to outguess their wily, talented ways. Every day is a learning experience that sharpens my wits. I have become a keener observer of the ways of Mother Nature—her sights, sounds, and quietness. Deep within me, I am in an awe of the universe and the way it works. At the same time, contentment permeates my body from a feeling or awareness of being a part in this grand scheme on this spinning planet.

WOODS

I like the woods and the smell of logs
And I like the smell of steaming bogs,
And the smell of the leaves that have fallen from the trees
And the smell of balsam on the breeze,
And the flowers of spring
And the frosted fern
And the wintergreen that grows on the burn.
I like to see the red bucks bed,
And the broken limbs where the bear has fed,
And the puff of feathers or pillow of hair
And to know the owls been feeding there.

And to see the grouse bud
And a fish hawk dine,
And the feed-tree of the porcupine.
I like the tracks of a lynx round a beaver house,
And the dainty tracks of a woodland mouse
And the padded path of a snowshoe hare
And the trail that leads to the foxes' lair,
And the wolf's long lope
And the minks short glide
And the icy Slope where the otters slide!
I like . . . I just like the woods!

From "Tales of the Trail"
by Theo Peacock, "The Haliburtan Trapper"

*   *   *

My retirement has given me more time to delve into the role of hunting. It truly is an exceedingly complicated, and controversial, subject. There are those that love it and those that hate it and a wide range in between.

My attempts to explain my perspective on hunting often fall on deaf ears. Sometimes, I find it similar to trying to convince my friend who has a phobia about cats that our pet poses no danger. Fear shuts down the rational mind and so does the intolerance that so often results from misunderstanding. Fortunately, I have experienced the opposite as well—numerous people who have little understanding of hunting have listened with interest and given me encouragement to convey my ideas.

Many who are ambivalent or say they have nothing against hunting are unknowingly supporting or promoting actions that discourage participation. For example, a friend told me that he will not allow a firearm, not even a toy one, in his house because of his wife's fear of guns. In his next breath, he stated he had nothing against hunting and in fact had enjoyed hunting with his father. He wished his son had a similar opportunity. Another person told me he has nothing against hunting if the cruelty to animals could be overcome. He did not realize that his concept of cruelty would mean no hunting and no slaughterhouses—in short, no meat at the table.

It is such an emotional topic that for years I avoided any discussion about hunting with nonhunting friends. In this age of political correctness with its emphasis on "how to win friends and influence people," we are taught to avoid personal conflicts and controversies—essential skills it seems to me if one is to succeed in this world.

Hunters complain among themselves about the antihunting feeling in society and the detrimental actions that evolve from it. But most do little to create a better understanding for nonhunters. After all, none of us want to irritate our friends. In fact, most of us are unable to articulate all the things that make up hunting or to describe adequately the value it has or our reasons for participating. Most of us do not fully comprehend it ourselves.

After years of silence and witnessing the tremendous drive to squeeze the life out of hunting, I feel compelled to try to create a better understanding between both the hunters and the nonhunters.

Hunting is a very significant aspect of our heritage. Considering that it has been an integral part of human nature for at least four hundred thousand years, it seems reasonable to agree with Freud and others that hunting is instinctual. Yet today, many people don't accept this possibility and believe it is wrong. By trying to bury it, they are not simply pushing aside nature but are wiping out parts of our very makeup along with activities that nourish our well-being. It has similarities to denying other emotions such as anger, sexual needs, the fight-or-flight response, or aggression. It is a fundamental psychological principle that whatever we disown or otherwise repress in our psyche becomes stronger and may eventually appear in a distorted or impulsive manner. When buried, emotions have a tendency to surface at some point in time in the form of inappropriate behaviour. We have a choice in how we view and handle such issues, and life is served better by understanding and developing emotions in a positive way.

*   *   *

The mysterious, paradoxical way in which nature works was illustrated for me when I was very young. One morning while walking down the path to the lake with my father, we encountered an ugly scene. A small snake was trying to subdue a frog. They were thrashing around violently. I was horrified at the struggle. My father explained that it was nature's way and, with his foot, eased the snake and frog out of sight into the ferns. That evening, the snake was visible again. The frog was partly swallowed but was still kicking for dear life. My father commented that anything with that much spirit deserved to live, so he killed the snake to free the frog and set the dead snake on a rock to feed the hawks and crows. I remember the incident vividly although I was only three years old.

I have thought about that episode often and have observed similar scenes over and over again. The frog, obviously, did not want to be food for the snake. He was fighting to save his life while the other fought to take it. To me, that incident is a metaphor for life. Nature appears very cruel in human terms, at least in terms of many humans. But what may seem cruel is nothing more than the flow of life, or nature's way. All life feeds on other life. There is pro and con to everything. There is a grand design, or order of things, that at times appears chaotic. It is a mystery and dilemma for us. Best we keep kicking because we never know when something or someone may come along to save us or do us in—especially if we are too greedy. Smart frogs learn to avoid snakes, and smart snakes to avoid humans—it's one of many ways in which survival of the fittest works.

Although nature often appears cruel, I believe this is a negative perception of something we do not understand. It is an undesirable perception, because if cruel is the way nature is perceived, that negativism seeps into the interpretation of many of life's challenging experiences, which results in missed positive effects and actually fosters feelings that are detrimental.

I don't know why nature works the way she does. We get trials and sorrow to make us stronger, pain to make us human, and a choice of attitudes that can transform hardships into challenges that are ultimately beneficial.

This was illustrated to me by my father's sudden death of a heart attack when he was twenty-nine and I was six. I could continue to view this as a tragedy or as an excuse for some difficulties in my life. However, for whatever reason, I have been blessed in many ways as a result of what happened. Many people stepped in to help me along the way. Also, I have more pleasant memories of my father than most whose fathers live a normal life span. Perhaps it is my nature to hunt for such things. I have related to my mother experiences with my father that while she knows them to be true still finds it unbelievable that I can remember events that occurred when I was a one-year-old.

The following further illustrates my early learning about paradoxes and hunters. My father's pioneer father died of a freak accident and left his family in extreme poverty. My father snared rabbits to ward off starvation and worked like a slave for many years. He had only a grade-four education but was a very knowledgeable, resourceful man. By the time he died, he had four children, had established a draying business, a delivery business, and shared mixed farming with my grandmother. He was also a pioneer in introducing beekeeping to the north. He loved animals and taught himself how to de-scent skunks to create loving pets. He was called upon to tend to sick farm animals or help with difficult births. I recall one cold March day, my father walking into the kitchen with a stray chicken he had found in a snowbank, half-frozen to death. My mother was not pleased at sharing her kitchen with a sick hen and three small children under four. She insisted he take the chicken to the stable where he made a bed for it in the hay by the horses. He tended that chicken night and day. To heal was a challenge. He was the same with humans. Yet he was a hunter.

I have found that those who are truly most loving of nature and animals are frequently hunters or have been.

We had a beautifully mounted buck's head in our living room, somewhat to my mother's chagrin. It did not fit with her idea of living room décor, and some of her friends were antihunting. But she respected and honoured my father's feelings. After all, what is wrong with displaying a beautiful trophy? For many, it has similarities akin to exhibiting antiques or artwork.

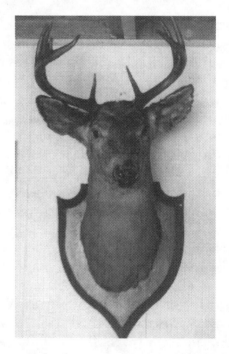

Deer head, Father's "work of art," now hangs at the cottage.

*   *   *

In this day of information technology, it is relatively easy to select data that misleads. Certainly, the behaviour of some hunters, particularly in past years, provides opponents with plenty of ammunition to depict hunting in an unfavourable light. But let's keep it in perspective—human conduct is disconcerting at times, whether in religion, sport, business, or everyday living.

When it comes to hunting, the often extracritical look taken is partially due to a human tendency to see implications in things we don't understand or like to admit about ourselves. A group of golfers at a tournament made critical statements to me about hunters' irresponsibility, citing the amount of drinking that takes place at a hunt camp as proof. After the tournament, this group had several drinks then drove off to a restaurant where they had more drinks before driving home. I have found other instances that indicate irresponsible behaviour occurs no more at hunt camps than in other activities.

Thomas Homer-Dixon makes an interesting point in his best seller *The Ingenuity Gap*. "We design our cities to block out the intrusions and fluctuations of the natural world so that they will work as smoothly and efficiently and with as little discomfort as possible," he writes. "But the disturbing result is that many urban residents no longer care about, or understand, or recognize the importance of the natural world. Our modern cities are vital engines of ingenuity and supply, producing much of what is best and most beautiful, but they also produce self-absorption, introversion, and hubris."

This hubris, or wanton disrespect towards hunting, is illustrated by the following composite of several conversations.

One day, I told my friends that I would be away the following week. Normally, I would let it go at that, knowing how they felt; but this time, I added, "I'm going hunting."

They asked how hunting could be justified—how could shooting a defenceless little animal be called a sport? Usually, I say nothing. It isn't worth the hassle. Hunting is an exceedingly complex and emotionally sensitive subject with no easy answers.

A significant difficulty is that the killing scene tugs at the heart of most. In our society, the word "kill" has taken on a totally negative connotation, similar to an unholy act. There are good reasons for this—wars, terrorism, and murders, for example. However, humans tend to paint with a broad brush, and this characteristic often results in unclear thinking and confused feelings. In this case, anything involving killing tends to get branded without considering that killing, other than that of human life, serves many important and necessary functions. As the great teacher/philosopher Joseph Campbell put it, "Life lives on life." The reconciliation to this condition is fundamental to all creation stories. Reconciliation of this condition is fundamental to the acceptance of hunting as an integral part of this wonder called life.

To live in a human body is to kill, like it or not. Killing is an integral part of the food chain. It is impossible to live on this earth without imposing death.

Everyone has killed what they consider nuisance creatures like mice, rats, and flies. We wash our hands to kill bacteria.

Every species feeds on other species, including us. We kill the animals we eat—beef, pork, lamb, chicken, turkey, and fish are consumed.

If killing is inherently wrong, then so is the design of our universe, which I do not believe.

This will be further explored in chapter 10, "On Killing."

*   *   *

Frequently, on returning from hunting, I am asked, "Did you get a moose?"

Unfortunately, I frequently have to reply no though I always add that we had a great time anyway and that I do not expect to always get a moose any more than I expect to catch a fish every time I go fishing. To be with friends, to have fun, to be close to nature are the main attractions.

Sometimes, that brings other questions. Why is killing so important to a hunter? Why not shoot with a camera and buy your food at the supermarket? A young lawyer once snapped at me, "Who needs it? I can buy whatever I require at the supermarket. The Bible states, 'Thou shalt not kill.' Who then kills the meat and poultry in the supermarket? I want to ask.

*   *   *

For several reasons, the hunt has more meaning or significance for participants when there is the possibility of harvesting the prey. Man has hunted since the beginning of time with this in mind. Success in catching your prey has similarities to hitting a home run or scoring a goal in hockey. It is part of the sport but not the most important part—at least it shouldn't be.

Hunting, in many respects, has an individual or private aspect similar to writing, painting, or other private acts. The details are not sufficiently interesting for someone to watch. Observing pictures is never the same as participating in the event and can be misleading. Pictures don't convey the deeper feeling and understanding that comes with participation. If a hunter succumbs to his ego and lets the kill become his most important goal, he too misses the full enjoyment of the process and observing nature in a way that promotes discovery of self.

The act of taking the life of an animal has an intrinsic meaning that a camera does not capture. A couple of observations indicate this is so. There are millions more hunters who harvest than those who only take a picture after they have spent days, or sometimes years, stalking their prey. Also, if you take a close look at the evidence, you will see, in general, that hunters contribute more to sustain wildlife than cameramen do. Hunters are in the forefront of establishing wildlife management practices and regulations based on good conservation principles in order to maintain the hunting resources. Refer to data in chapter 3, "Benefits of Hunting," for evidence that supports this claim. Hunters through their organizations (such as Ontario Federation of Anglers and Hunters, Canadian Wildlife Federation, hundreds of local fish and game associations, and private hunting clubs) have put millions of dollars and acres into wildlife habitat and have been doing so for years. They are also the organizations that lobbied governments to separate licence fees from general revenue and to use this money (millions of dollars in Ontario) for hunting—and fishing-conservation purposes. Individuals and their organizations stock, reintroduce species, and improve habitat for cover and feeding. Overall, they give more than they take and provide an environment where both the hunted and nonhunted can survive, even thrive. Harvesting also contributes to sustaining healthy animals. Culling the herd has many benefits through survival of the fittest and reduces problems that come with overpopulation. Many of those who hunt with a camera began by experiencing hunting to take a life for food.

In a civilized and cultivated country, wild animals only
continue to exist at all when preserved by the sportsmen.
—Theodore Roosevelt

*　　*　　*

There are several reasons why killing and preparing your own food is a worthy experience. It has similarities to painting a picture or sewing a dress. There is something about the doing that brings satisfaction. We have all experienced this from making something we can just as easily buy. But there is an even greater significance that is tough to explain.

There's something undeniably primal about hunting for food. It promotes a sense of rugged self-sufficiency. It takes you into the fields and forests and fresh air. Best of all is the thrill of the hunt. After hours of planning and preparation, you never know when you're going to hit the mother lode. There are few events that can produce the depth and mixture of feelings—anticipation, awe, fear, excitement, mastery, power, superiority, gratitude, joy, revulsion, sadness, humbleness, and an awareness of life. It seems to satisfy a prehistoric urge. You can't say this about shopping at the supermarket.

In an article in the *Globe And Mail*, Philippe Caron writes that after he had killed his first chicken and watched it twitch violently in his hands before he cleaned, cooked, and ate it, "I had never tasted a more flavourful chicken in my life. I knew I had learned something important that day—something easily lost in our modern world: The further we are separated from unmediated, tangible experience, the further we get from knowing ourselves and the world we live in. Did I enjoy the experience—not really but it was refreshingly, terribly real."

A dose of reality is often beneficial. Reality therapy is a technique used in psychotherapy to reduce the need for medicinal dosages, such as antidepressants, pain relievers, sleeping pills, and a host of other drugs. I think most of us have an inkling of this phenomenon, but a grasp of this as it relates to Caron's statement or a wilderness experience may be more elusive. However, more and more is being written that highlights this phenomenon.

In chapter 2, "A Mysterious Message and Ensuing Information," I mention Dr. David Cumes who in his book *Inner Passages, Outer Journey* advocates wilderness experience for healing and the discovery of self for those who have the courage to go there. He points out that it was not so long ago that we were all rooted in wilderness as hunter-gatherers. Like Caron, he suggests that something is lost in our modern world—that the further we are separated from the natural world, the further we get from knowing ourselves.

In this world, one species exists by the demise of another. Even our immune system is based on this principle. This is the way the world works. This is the way our Creator set it up. If man derives benefit by hunting, so be it as long as it is done within the law, with good conservation principles of sustaining the herd, and with respect for others.

* * *

Several times, I have been told that serial killers often start by killing small creatures, the inference being that such an activity contributes to brutality. People tell me they have seen interviews with murderers who claim their hunting upbringing contributed to their downfall. It is suggested that we should never teach killing because once you learn to kill one thing, it is easier to progress to the next. Surely, if this were true, the result would have been a proliferation of murderers and serial killers instead of hunter-gatherers.

A warped mind is a warped mind, and we seldom understand why.

Traditionally, youths were taught to hunt to develop their progress towards responsible adulthood. Generally, people who learn to shoot and kill animals are much less likely to act in an irresponsible way with weapons and towards the world around them.

* * *

Many people say hunters should at least give animals a fighting chance—use a bow and arrow or black powder. My take is that I want to use the most-advanced legal weapon to effect the quickest, cleanest kill possible. But I have great respect for the skill of others who have successfully mastered those less-advanced tools. I don't believe any of us would agree to revert to sticks and stones to give the animal a fair chance. There are other ways to accomplish this. What we really should be concerned about is giving the animals a chance to sustain themselves. This is done by providing habitat, hunting seasons, bag limits, and the host of other gaming regulations that regulate the sport.

Some people question the assertion that hunting is instinctual. They claim not to have that instinct, and they don't see it in others. I suggest that instincts may be like muscles, the sex drive, or aggressive tendencies—appearing stronger in some than others. Perhaps the hunting instinct is more a masculine trait. We may not be aware of our instincts, but that doesn't mean that they are not there. Instincts, like muscles, atrophy if not used. However, a special exercise to develop a hidden muscle will add to overall performance. Back problems, for example, are often alleviated by special exercises that strengthen muscles unknown to the patient. Similarly, therapists and peak-performance coaches bring to light latent talents in individuals that do much to empower them. There is growing evidence that many allergies and other sicknesses are due, at least in part, to modern cleanliness habits and fast fixes that do not give our immune system the exercise needed for strengthening and development.

*　　*　　*

Most people live in the environment of urban centres, away from the truly natural world. They manicure their trees and lawns, even at their cottages equipped with indoor plumbing, electricity, and all the comforts of home. They want to live in a world where there are no black flies, pests, or inconveniences. Food is obtained already packaged. They view animals as cute little creatures as seen in cartoons and movies. They don't like pain and don't want to see pain. They have begun to regard nature as nothing more than scenery and never part of themselves. They feel little connection to the natural world or their impact on it. They pay no attention to the loss of habitat and pollution that their consumptive lifestyle imposes on the animal world. They do not see themselves and their lifestyle as being, by far, the foremost killer of wild animals on this planet.

Many people claim that the only reason animals hunt is for food. They fail to observe that even when their bellies are full, dogs and cats continue to hunt. These animals love to hunt and sometimes play with their prey. So do wild animals. We have coyotes in our neighbourhood that kill pet cats and squirrels. Some individuals were of the opinion that if they lovingly provided food to the coyotes, they would stop hunting and killing other animals. The "full belly" theory didn't work, and the availability of food attracted even more coyotes. Only after a satisfying hunt does the animal rest.

> *Psychological sustenance comes from the mental, social,*
> *cultural, and spiritual rewards of hunting and*
> *eating the animals killed.*
> —Dr. Terry Quinney,
> Provincial Coordinator of Fish and Wildlife Services

*   *   *

Skinning and dressing an animal is not everyone's idea of fun, even among hunters. However, many do get great satisfaction from their surgical-type skills.

"How awful." Many wince when they see the realities of a slaughterhouse.

However, we should be grateful for the process and the kind of people who are willing to do this type of work because we do need people to prepare our food.

A recent discussion on Toronto's most popular talk show was revealing and representative of many of the attitudes I encounter. A respected moderator expressed abhorrence for anyone who could kill and skin a wild animal. His perception was supported by an overwhelming majority of callers who seemed to feel that wild animals are more sacred than cattle, sheep, pigs, and domestic animals we raise for food. Several callers suggested that hunting made firearms' ownership acceptable whereas fear of the guns should be promoted to discourage gun ownership. Callers who tried to explain otherwise were belittled.

I suggested to the moderator that he compare the life of a wild animal with the life of a domestic animal raised for food and asked which life he would prefer for himself. Would it be the life of the domestic animal, confined to a pen and often not seeing the light of day? These animals are herded and sometimes injured during transportation to the slaughterhouse where they are killed by the hands that fed them. Or would he prefer the life of the wild animal, free to roam with choices in his natural environment and an opportunity to outwit hunters?

On average, only about 5 percent of game animals are harvested by hunters. I know which I would select, but he didn't answer.

*   *   *

We work hard and enjoy the excitement of our hunts. Animals are not that easy to outsmart. Hunting makes the breed grow stronger in many ways. Occasionally, we get a glimpse of bears that we wish were not there. They disturb the moose and frequently kill their calves. Having a moose or a bear present itself is an extraordinary experience as is preparing them for the dinner table.

After much contemplation about hunting, I now see more clearly something I have always felt—the act of preparing our food is indeed a sacred one; and when properly completed within the context of a wilderness hunt, it brings many benefits to the participant. The hunter and hunted grow wiser and stronger.

Gary Zukav, heralded as one of the finest interpreters of the new physics and who is considered equally conversant with the human spirit, writes, "Only when we see through eyes that lack reverence does the feeding of one animal on another appear to be a cruel system instead of one where there is a natural give and take and sharing of energies. This is ecology." I believe acceptance of this philosophy is an important step to the way in which we perceive our own misfortunes. This understanding can help alleviate negative thoughts and feelings that contribute to unhappiness, ill health, anger, and violence.

I have stated this throughout this book but feel the concept is sufficiently important to warrant reiteration. An appreciation of the reality of our food chain and the flow of life that is learned in a wilderness experience has many demonstrated benefits. When a person shoots and kills an animal, life and death become very real. The experience can have transformative qualities or act like an awareness seed that grows and blossoms with time.

Contrast this with many of today's youths whose exposure to killing, starting at a very young age, is the playing of computer games in which the objective is to destroy. There is no real consequence to killing in these games. Players, in fact, are rewarded for their ability to destroy. There is ample evidence that such youths are prone to developing an unrealistic perception of life and death. Their feelings are dulled. Therefore, they are more apt to inflict harm in real life, intentionally or unintentionally. We are witnessing a tremendous number of troubled youths and adults. Often, they are treated with medication. There is now much concern over the side effects of these drugs, which further dull feelings, judgement, and, in a growing number of cases, actually result in other illnesses.

There is growing evidence that a reconnection with Mother Earth through wilderness and hunting experiences has empowering results, including a measurable reduction in drug use and violent behaviour. An individual gains a more realistic expectation about life, a more balanced outlook.

Hugh Fraser, the founder of the Fraser Recovery Program (a program that has had great success rehabilitating young drug addicts) says, "I discovered that the woods, with no TV or radio, that the wilderness was doing for them exactly what drugs were doing but in a positive way . . . One guy said to me, 'Hugh, I never felt so good. I'm at peace.'"

The book *The Sacred Hunt* by Dr. Randall Eaton refers to a recent program in the United States that took one thousand violent youths over a five-year period into the wilderness under conditions that demanded they scrounge their food, or their meals, from Mother Nature. Some developed ways to capture and kill small animals and other creatures to satisfy their hunger. This, in some mysterious way, resulted in 85 percent of them reducing their violent behaviour upon returning to their normal environment. Unfortunately, this program was discontinued because of some people's concerns over the killing of the small animals.

The Management section of a national newspaper recently contained an article about wilderness survival courses in which business executives engage "to gain leadership skills, self-confidence and stress management skills." The article described an incident in which one of the students, while being taught to light a fire without matches, asked, "What would happen if he couldn't get a fire lit?"

The leader, Dr. Gino Ferri, answered, "Don't do it, you don't eat."

Imagine a similar situation in which a person is being taught how to kill and prepare an animal for food was told, "Don't do it, you don't eat." Properly done, this might go a long way towards connecting people to Mother Earth and the food chain. Hunting traditionally provided this. Dr. Ferri simulates this in one of his survival programs in which the only food are ants, grasshoppers, or tiny creatures that participants are taught how to catch.

*   *   *

Let us not overlook the fact that people matter more than animals. Sometimes, it takes an extreme illustration to bring this home. If both a child and an animal were in danger of being killed, and you could save only one of them, which would you save?

This was brought to my attention at an early age. My mother frequently read to us when we were young, and I recall vividly the impact of a book called *The Yearling*. It caused me to think much more than did the book or movie *Bambi*. *The Yearling* is the story of a young boy raised in the backwoods who adopted a fawn when it had lost its mother to nature. The boy and fawn played and slept together. He loved the deer deeply, and the deer seemed to adopt the boy as his mother. As the fawn grew, so did its appetite and ability to jump fences to eat the garden vegetables. The father warned the boy that the fawn had to be kept out of the garden. When the father again found the deer in the garden, he shot it. The boy was heartbroken and angry. How could his father be so cruel to coldheartedly kill this loving pet that had meant so much to him? I went to my room to hide my own tears. My mother sensed my upset and explained the reality behind the act, which was that the deer was destroying the family's only food supply. I understood the rationale but struggled with the feelings that came with the images in my mind.

A friend of mine who is not a hunter told me that he was reading *Bambi* to his grandson who had commented on "those bad hunters." I said that I hoped he would also read something to his grandson to provide another perspective and mentioned *The Yearling*. A mother disagreed with me saying that the boy could learn about the harshness of life when he was older. My comment that beliefs are predominantly established by the age of six did not sit well.

Walt Disney and *Bambi* have misled many of us. Every species has a survival instinct and struggles to avoid death, but they do not talk like humans about death and pain. Nor do they have the thinking capacity of humans or the ability to create and use tools.

*   *   *

After observing nature's system for many years, I conclude that there is a superior intelligence that has a hand in the structure and its processes. This Creator appears to be sufficiently thoughtful to give creatures a built-in quality that allows them to tolerate pain. For example, a deer shot with the quietness of an arrow often flinches no more than it would from a fly bite. The animal will continue eating and fraternizing with other deer till it tires and drops dead. The loud noise of a rifle shot, on the other hand, has a greater immediate impact—the animal's fright in this case is its fear of noise.

High school biology students use frogs to learn that these creatures have a very rudimentary nervous system. It is reasonable to believe that animals have a more highly developed nervous system than frogs but one that is surely less than humans'.

It appears to me that many people attribute feelings to creatures as if they were humans, and in my opinion, much of the energy spent anguishing over pain perceived in animals would be better directed towards methods that enhance our own animal-like pain-reducing capabilities.

*   *   *

We naturally form attachment to animals, some more than others. I was made vividly aware of this in the rural environment in which I grew up. We were exposed to the need to take the life of certain creatures—a chicken for Sunday dinner, a groundhog or a squirrel for destroying our food or flowers, the starlings and blackbirds who were a nuisance, a sick or hurt animal. But there were rules and conventions on what not to kill. For example, the robins, the goldfinches, the hummingbirds, the chickadees, and the woodpeckers were treasures to behold.

*   *   *

When I was a youngster, my aunt would call my mother around Thanksgiving to invite us to their farm on the day my uncle would be killing his pigs. My mother and my aunt stayed in the house, but the boys were naturally expected to join my uncle in lighting the fire that heated a giant iron pot of water and witness him shoot the pig, cut its throat to bleed it, hang it to gut it, and drop it in the pot of boiling water to clean it of hair in preparation for the meat-cutting table. I recall the first time I attended the event. When we reached the pigpen, my uncle handed me a pail and, in a serious tone, told me, "It is your job to catch the squeal."

They all laughed when I stood, feet apart and braced, ready with the pail. Pigs often squeal at death—something akin to the chicken that runs around with its head cut off. The joke is on us if we interpret this the wrong way.

Usually, chicken was planned for dinner, so the next item on the agenda was to hunt down a suitable chicken among the many pecking about the yard. Chickens weren't penned up the way they are today. Of course, not any chicken would do. You tracked down a "clucker." My aunt was an expert at this. Chickens cluck naturally to announce when they have laid an egg while "cluckers" do a lot of clucking but don't produce eggs. You may have noticed humans with the same characteristics. Once the clucker was identified, she was chased, grabbed, had her head cut off at the chopping block, and then prepared for the roasting pot.

I was cautioned not to become a clucker. When I hunt, I always stop every few steps and listen for "cluckers"—animals that make a noise. The wisest animals keep silent, and consequently, I pass by.

After everything was cleaned up, my uncle would take a piece of straw and blow up the pig's bladder to make us a football. Then my cousins, brothers, and uncle would have a game of football—similar to soccer. We couldn't afford the luxury of a real football, so it was quite a treat. After the game, tired and hungry, we sat at the table and gave a long prayer of thanks. My aunt was very religious. Then we feasted.

Only recently have I begun to fully appreciate the importance of this event and often wonder why my aunt and uncle made a point of inviting us to partake in the slaughter. I now believe that they felt it was important for children to experience the realities of the food chain in a positive way. In the rural setting, this aspect occurred naturally and at a very early age. This is no longer so because of the massive movement from the rural to the urban centres. However, with a little thought and effort, there are ways to capture this beneficial experience.

We were also encouraged to hunt and fish.

In his best seller *Iron John*, Robert Bly points out that many boys become fascinated with hunting, make small bows and arrows, form hunting bands, shoot rabbits or birds, and enthusiastically bring home a dead cottontail or bird. Bly's words ring true to my experiences. He points out that many women, and some men, feel that a boy's hunting instinct is deplorable and that he should be educated out of it and want the boy to bypass hunting and go directly to ethics. Bly claims that the trouble with such a bypass is that the boy mythologically misses living through a past history of joyful hunting in which man's emotional and even his religious life resonates to the empty spaces of forest and plain. Bly says, "If a shaming mother or father blocks a boy from living that time through, he will never arrive at contemporary time." This will often degenerate into self-loathing, self-contempt, and violence.

Hunting provides an environment for learning various aspects of life—geography, map reading, conservation, animal behaviour, boating, wilderness survival, safe use of dangerous tools, and responsibility. Similar to life itself, enjoying the process and learning from the experience is where the gold or silver lining is discovered.

We all make mistakes or, on an impulse, do something we regret. These are usually wake-up calls to tweak us to our responsibilities. They are part of learning. The various activities involved in hunting provide many such opportunities.

I mentioned earlier that I have a concern about youth involvement in violence and shootings and that the experience of killing an animal often brings home a reality that video games mask. The first time a youth kills an animal often causes a change in him, an awakening if you will. The animal doesn't quietly succumb or come back to life as they do in video games and so many television shows. There is growing evidence that the experience of killing an animal reduces violent behaviour in many youths.

The following incident illustrates the type of experience to which I refer though not easy to explain. Thirty years ago when my oldest son was fourteen, I gave him a BB gun. He was thrilled with his possession and all but slept with it. One day while out in the woods with his cousins and brother, and to demonstrate his skills, he shot at and hit a squirrel. It fell to the ground and cried. He was horrified at what he had done. His younger brother had to pick up the gun to make the final shot to put the squirrel away. Tim never used his gun again and later became a vegetarian. I heard about the squirrel incident years later. Tim is a sensitive, intelligent, fine young man of whom we are proud. He tells me he occasionally still thinks of the incident with an element of regret. I have suggested to him that I hope he revaluates the experience someday from a different perspective. I think it would be healthy for him to partake in a hunt with the reverence it deserves. It was rewarding for me after several years of doubting its value, and I think it would be for him. But my son knows that I accept that his decision as his own. I also know that he respects my position and does not approve of the antihunters and government actions that unnecessarily deter enjoyment of the activity. Tim also feels an experience such as his might well act as a wake-up call for many youths and foster a more realistic and responsible attitude towards violence, life, and death.

* * *

Two years after I wrote the foregoing and thirty years after the above incident, Tim, age forty-five, asked his brother Richard to take him and his friend Dereck for a holiday at our remote cottage that Tim had not visited for twenty years.

* * *

When he returned home from that outing, he called to let me know how much they had enjoyed the cottage, its wilderness setting, and their experiences there. His brother had taken a .22 rifle and a couple of replica muzzleloaders (a firearm that is loaded down the muzzle with black powder and projectile and was superseded by cartridge firearms in the 1800s). For some completely unplanned reason, Tim and his friend who had never fired a gun wanted to try firing them. Richard gave them instructions on the safety measures involved in handling and shooting a gun then set up a fixed target. Tim's friend was thrilled by his newly acquired shooting skill with the .22, like a child with his first success at riding a bike. Next came another challenge, shooting at a swinging tin can attached to a tree branch. Later while walking down a trail, they saw some partridge, and Tim shot one with his brother's .22! Dereck also shot one and kept firing at it as it flailed about, wings flapping. Richard explained that the first shot had killed the partridge, and a bird normally acted that way for a short time after death, and there was a risk of ruining good meat with unnecessary shots. Fortunately, no meat was damaged because Dereck, as if by nature, was such a fine marksman that only the head was hit. They shot two more partridge and could have easily killed more, but Richard told them to leave the rest of the partridge. He showed them an easy way to clean one and prepare it for cooking. Tim and his friend did the others and seemed to gain something by getting their hands awash in the blood and guts inherent in the process. Tim, the vegetarian, cooked the partridge. He then ate a full-size portion of meat! He and his friend loved the taste and were thrilled with the entire experience. They also caught fish, cleaned and cooked them, and thoroughly enjoyed the deliciousness of this meal. For Tim, the partridge hunt and feast had been the highlight of the trip.

Tim and Dereck, as a matter of fact, regretted having to leave for home and requested that Richard plan to act as their guide every year for the next ten years in an autumn trip to the cottage. They also talked about inviting another friend and his girlfriend.

Over the dinner table, they discussed the possible meanings of their wilderness experience. The events had been spontaneous for all of them although in Tim's case, he said that he had often thought that it might be beneficial for him to revisit the scene of his boyhood experience. They wondered about the element of sadness that they felt over the death of the birds and also the same sadness they noticed in the eyes of Richard, "the Hunter." They wondered if it reflected a subconscious reverence for animals, the universe, and thankfulness for the food provided. They also commented on the wisdom of not taking more from the environment than needed. They agreed that they would never again look at store-bought meat in the same way. They agreed that the hunting process was so much more humane than the processes involved in the raising of domestic animals for death in the abattoir.

You may wonder if I am "putting words in their mouths." I assure you that I am not. In fact, my sons have been party to discussions that led to the writing of this book.

In the above story, I mention the joy that came with the skill of learning to shoot at targets as well as the precautions and responsibility needed for proper use. I experienced a similar learning experience with bows and arrows at a resort in Mexico where I was vacationing with a group. The resort offered several events of interest, including lessons on shooting with a bow and arrow. Although most of the group were antigun and had no experience in shooting, they signed up, and I went with them. I was abhorred when one adult loaded an arrow into his bow and pointed it at one of his friends in fun. I stepped into my instructor mode and warned him about the danger of such an act. I also took the opportunity to explain that owning a gun or a weapon of any kind requires that one must be better informed. Perhaps a more significant observation is that the group thoroughly enjoyed shooting at targets, and a competition based on target shooting skills grew naturally out of the experience.

*   *   *

Here is another example of a type of learning experience that occurs but perhaps is not commonly recognized. We had a pet squirrel at the cottage. The young son of a fellow hunter joined us for a hunt. I warned him, "Don't shoot the pet squirrel."

"Don't shoot any squirrels, only partridge," his grandfather added firmly.

One morning, I heard a bang and another boy say, "Good shot." I went to check, expecting to see a partridge, but there lay the pet squirrel.

"I asked you not to shoot the pet squirrel. Let me have the gun," I said angrily.

The boy's father and his grandfather apologized and said that they had been having problems with him. "He won't listen," they apologized further.

One of the other hunters felt that I was overreacting. After all, the squirrel was a wilderness animal and could just as easily have met his fate in the jaws of a weasel. I asked the father if I could talk to his son to explain my concern, which was that he had ignored the request of the owner of the property and of his grandfather. His father encouraged me to do so and reiterated, "He pays no attention to me." I had noticed this on several occasions when the lad was being careless around the boats.

So I had a chat with him in private and explained the importance of obeying rules. I pointed out that the squirrel was a trusting pet that another person had spent hours taming. In consideration of others, his grandfather and me, he should not have done what he did. I went on to suggest that by his lack of consideration of others, he had been lucky this time. He had only killed a pet squirrel, but if he continued to disregard his father's advice about rules for driving a car, for instance, he might wound or kill a human. I suggested that he accept the experience as a wake-up call and gave him back his gun.

I suggest there are some hunters who should show more respect for the feelings of others, especially nonhunters, and make an effort to find words that could gain sympathy.

Several years later, I asked the boy's father if he observed any behavioural changes in his son that might be attributable to the foregoing. He said he had discussed the incident with the boy who had commented that I was right. The father further said that he had noticed an improvement in his son's attitude. He was treating life more seriously—for example, his decision to go to university. This may have been normal maturing. We do not know. However, the boy's father felt the incident had been a positive experience. Last year, the boy, now a fine young man, took a week off from his studies to join us in a hunt. I think we both look forward to future hunts together.

Here is another event that amused my family while providing valuable lessons about life. It is especially pertinent to my comments about fear. Perhaps it will be of interest to you too. When my boys were very young, we took our cat to the cottage. The cat was in his glory. There were so many little creatures to hunt and chase. One chipmunk delighted in teasing him by sneaking up to him, chattering, then darting up a tree to jeer at him, just out of reach. One day while we were sitting out on the deck down the path, the cat strutted with the chipmunk by the tail to show us his cleverness. My mother later said the cat looked like me when I strutted home with my first hunting success.

"He killed the little chipmunk!" the boys cried out.

"I don't think so," I commented and went up to the cat who was anticipating that I would reward him for his achievement.

He was completely surprised when I took the chipmunk from him. The only thing more surprised was the chipmunk, whose little body was shivering with terror. The boys held the cat out of view while I set the chipmunk on a branch in a little clump of cedars. He was petrified and could hardly hang on. I was concerned he might fall from his hiding spot. But he lay there for at least an hour while the cat searched high and low for his trophy. Finally, the chipmunk was gone. In the days that followed, I saw him several times, but he had learned his lesson and stayed away from the cat.

*   *   *

The paralyzing fear I witnessed in that chipmunk has caused me to ponder many times on fear that is so frequently seen in man and other animals. We are warned by experts about the insidious and unhealthy effects of fear on people and their relationships. Too often, it results in people organizing to promote their cause and impose restrictions on others. It is the basis of much intolerance and discrimination. The fear of "the gun" that has been created is a factor that negatively impacts on participation in the sport of hunting. Many people with no hands-on experience have a hard time understanding that a gun is a tool that can be used for good or bad. Somehow, they have been conditioned into believing that there is something sinister about a gun. For many people, hunting is an irrational fear, a phobia. Dr. Phil often discusses the negative aspects of fear on his popular television program and in his books. Many benefits accrue to us when we become aware of our irrational fears, become more realistic, and subdue them.

Hunting experiences can be a significant aid in fostering more realistic perspectives.

Here is an example of misdirected fear in action. My wife was raised in a small town on a lake. She wanted to learn to swim, but her mother who had an exaggerated fear of drowning would not let her go near the water. When, at the age of nine, my wife went into the water at a beach to play with her friends, she waded into a spot deeper than expected and had a near-drowning experience. The average child responds to this type of situation by learning to swim. But because my wife's mother feared water, she used the incident to further develop an irrational fear in my wife. This fear of drowning deterred my wife from partaking in or enjoying many activities, including a healthful exercise that is available in our swimming pool or even a trip in a boat. Because we recognized that thinking tends to get passed on, we took special steps to ensure this irrational fear was not passed on to our children. They were taught to swim and enjoy the water at an early age.

You may have observed that this pattern occurs all too frequently. A mother who is bitten by a dog or another animal when young develops a fear of the animal. She passes this fear along to her children who panic whenever one comes near.

People often go "squirrelly," an old hunter explained. Watch how a squirrel acts due to fear of a weasel. Many animals react in a similar way—the human animal too.

The word "squirrelly" means confused thinking or acting without all faculties. For those who have never been exposed to a squirrel-and-weasel scenario, let me describe it. The squirrel is superior in many ways to the weasel; he is bigger and is more skilled in a tree, climbing out on branches and jumping great distances from one to another. Despite his superior capabilities, the squirrel is not safe from the weasel. The weasel is able to catch him for dinner. This is how it happens. The squirrel senses danger and races up a tree. The weasel runs up after him. The squirrel leaps to another tree. The weasel then scrambles down the tree and goes to the one where the squirrel rests. The weasel starts up that tree, and the squirrel jumps to another. This procedure is repeated until all the weasel has to do is appear at the bottom of the tree, and the squirrel leaps in panic to the next tree. The squirrel, in his frenzy, loses his strength and becomes paralyzed for easy picking. Fear causes him to go "squirrelly" with disastrous consequences. As strange as it may seem, his overconcern for safety confuses him so that he loses his natural abilities and rushes into inappropriate behaviour that brings about the very thing he is trying to avoid. If he maintained his composure and wits, he would be able to cope and probably overcome the danger.

A lot can be discovered about humans by observing animals in a wilderness setting while sitting quietly, watching, and contemplating— especially with proper mentorship. The thinking process and knowledge spills over into all aspects of life. Good mentorship by hunters needs greater attention, in my opinion, similar to that provided by native elders.

*   *   *

Surely, fear should be a concern for us. Many claim that we are becoming an excessively fearful society, which accounts for many problems. For example, according to Statistics Canada's recent health survey, phobias (fears) affect 6.6 percent of adult Canadians. That is a stunning number when compared with 5 percent of the population with heart disease. Dr. Martin Anthony, director of the Anxiety Treatment and Research Centre in Hamilton, believes phobia sufferers are underreported and says, "If you add up all the types of phobias, it would affect 15 to 25 percent of the population." The Anxiety Disorders Association of Canada has a similar estimate.

According to researchers/psychologists, and I think most people have observed this, one of the problems with irrational fears is they interfere with enjoyment of life. Excessive fear results in anxiety and stress, which contribute significantly to colds, heart disease, strokes, and, in fact, all illnesses as well as to flawed thinking. Much evidence is available that when retained unnecessarily, fear creates poisons in our bodies enough to kill a rat, enough to contribute to many illnesses including cancer. It also is a major ingredient of anger, which exacerbates the foregoing and is a factor in crime. A growing number of studies point to the extent of these connections.

There is much evidence that hunting can extend the boundaries of awareness if one is open to searching for such evidence. It can make one more accepting of the challenges in life, thus reducing frustrations, hurts, fears, anger, and their devastating effects.

*   *   *

A friend commented that from his observations, many hunters do not seem to experience the things I mention. I'm sure this is true in many cases. However, in all experiences, the individual plays a significant role in the extent of his participation and what he gains from it. This friend is a staunch supporter of his church, so I pointed out that many people do not see church attendees experiencing all of the goodness and love that is supposed to develop there. In fact, throughout history, religions have, at times, been banned because of wars and other problems associated with religion. I asked him how he felt about that. He said he realized going to church was not a cure-all, but to eliminate churches was not the answer—the good aspects of religions needed promotion and erroneous activities corrected.

Precisely, I agreed.

To ban religions would be like throwing out the baby along with the bathwater. I don't support such actions. In my opinion, it is never genuine religion that has hindered man's progress but the selfish priestcraft of politics that have done so in the name of God. Too often, leaders become overly self-righteous and find a platform of belief from which to launch crusades to control those whose ideas differ from their own.

*   *   *

I have occasionally told friends that I wish they had experienced Dr. Randall Eaton's presentation *The Sacred Hunt* to a group of over one thousand hunters in Toronto in 2001. He brought tears to the eyes of many because he expressed something they felt but were unable to articulate.

I have used quotes extensively throughout this document because they helped me so much in clarifying and developing a better understanding in myself. In my searching, I uncovered thinkers and experts who express the complexities of hunting more effectively than me. They are highly educated, informed people who have studied the subject. Their words have also helped add credibility to my claims in my discussions with others. Here are a few more examples.

In the introduction to his book *The Sacred Hunt: Hunting as a Sacred Path*, Dr. Eaton claims that the tragic state of the earth, the creatures, and our bodies originate from a fearful state of mind. It is a universal law that what we fear will come to us. As strange as that may seem, we create the reality we fear. Fearful thoughts create fearful consequences. Fearful thoughts create a poison world and spread poisons into our bodies.

Eaton says the solution for the world does not lie in technology but in ourselves. It all comes down to choosing between love and fear, spirit or ego. He states, "In matters of the heart, hunters are at the forefront of reversing the trend. Ducks Unlimited, for example, has purchased eight million acres of habitat in North America. And they began doing it sixty years ago before anyone had heard of ecology. That is honouring life and putting money where your heart is."

He calls it a tragedy that antihunters are spending hundreds of millions of dollars annually to stop hunting, pointing out that hunters are compelled to respond by wasting enormous amounts of money and energy that could be spent helping the earth. He refers to it as a stupid war that would not exist if all of us participated directly in the most fundamental processes of life that we have lost touch with due to the realities of life.

Writes Eaton, "I am more convinced than ever that properly done, the taking of a life that feeds us is transformative. And so it is that we need to promote hunting precisely because it connects people to the earth, the creatures, the human community and the Divine. Nothing is more important for our young people, especially boys. Girls understand the connection between blood, life and the life force. Boys need to learn it. Hunting is one of a very few paths in which humans may link up the instinctive with the spiritual and discover the fullness of their own being."

James Swan in his book *The Sacred Art of Hunting* presents an anecdote that illustrates what hunting can convey. It is the story of the first deer harvested by a friend who happens to be both a counsellor and a former priest. The friend narrates the story. He points out that he had hunted squirrels and rabbits when he was a kid. Then he went off to college and the ministry and forgot about hunting. After a few years, he decided he wanted to work more with people as a healer than as a priest and so went back to school and got a degree in psychology. One of his buddies from high school invited him to go deer hunting, and the first morning, a four-point buck stepped out in front of him. Although he was shaking with excitement, he dropped the buck with one shot. He describes that at first, he felt a wave of sadness—the deer was so beautiful. Then, gradually, he thought about what had happened and came to realize he was finally being honest about killing the meat he ate and knelt down and said a prayer. He says, "It was the most profound spiritual experience I had ever felt."

The following is an explanation on the meaning of hunting by Ortega y Gasset, the highly respected Spanish thinker, professor, and writer. In his book *Meditations on Hunting*, he says our hearts vacillate between a yearning for novelties and a constant eagerness to turn back. In history, the latter predominates, and happiness has generally been thought to be simplicity and primitivism. Man feels happy when he dreams of stripping off the oppressive present and floating in a simpler element. "Although it is inadmissible to completely transfer our existence to a previous form of life," Ortega says, "why not do so partially for a while in order to rest the painful existence of the here and now? This would be a great diversion . . . if we move backward, towards more and more generic ways of being a man. This is the reason people hunt."

In an article in the *Globe and Mail* (November 29, 1997), David Bercuson and Barry Cooper, professors of history and political science at the University of Calgary, made several compelling arguments in support of hunting. The following is the gist of their case:

1. Most hunters learn to hunt with their fathers and other males they admire. By and large, hunting is a male ritual. For most hunters, the point of hunting is obvious. For those who have never hunted, it is simply unintelligible. But that is true of all rituals and sports.
2. The male shift in their use of free time from hunting is not without its costs. Obviously, there will be a price paid by the geese and wild animals when they run out of food and starve or turn to the farmers' crops for food.
3. The animal rights advocates have yet to acknowledge their responsibility for wildlife overpopulation.
4. According to Leon Craig, a political philosopher at the University of Alberta, attacks on hunters and hunting are also attacks on manliness. Worse, he says, it is "the legitimization of the weakness of men." Hunting is a civil way for people to use their aggressive instincts and feel good about themselves. When that feeling is suppressed or gone, the remaining sensitive guys will easily be displaced by those who may be strong but turn their aggression to injurious acts.

*   *   *

I am sympathetic to those sensitive, thoughtful people who choose not to hunt. Although I think many would benefit from a proper hunting experience, I accept that the decision is theirs to make.

I have several friends who were hunters but gave it up for a variety of reasons. They claim they do not miss hunting. Some now hunt with a camera. They don't feel the need to kill animals. This seems to be quite common in this busy urban world; but it does not take away the subtle benefits they gained, perhaps unconsciously, while hunting.

CHAPTER 9

Ethics in hunting

The ethics involved in hunting presents a dilemma. Governments are being pushed to legislate hunting ethics.

The debate rages over the ethics of various methods of hunting, even among hunters. It is an exceedingly complex issue, without a simple right or wrong. Some hunters, for example, feel it is unethical to bait bears with food yet don't equate planting wild rice, using decoys and duck calling, or fishing as similar forms of baiting. Calling moose or wild turkey is also a form of baiting. Some feel it is acceptable to hunt with bow and arrow but not with a gun. Some feel birds must be flushed and shot only when flying; others who hunt partridge in heavy bush disagree. The list is never ending. It is almost impossible to find a hunting method that everyone can agree is ethical. To the antihunters, none of it is ethical.

Can politicians realistically establish hunting ethics? I say no for several reasons.

Hunting is dependent on the situation. Those who understand hunting know this. It is analogous to trying to regulate ethics in the bedroom. Individual situations, beliefs, and choices are too varied. Nonetheless, nurturing proper behaviour is a part of hunting, just as it should be in all walks of life.

Each time a hunter decides to chase and kill, he must balance many factors, many of which involve ethical dilemmas. For example, is the animal in range? Is it legal to kill? Can it be retrieved? Sometimes, a hunter doesn't pull the trigger because he feels an affinity with the animal at that moment.

The nature of politicians in government is such that in the process of forming regulations they solicit and act on, opinions from all sources including nonhunters in this case and antihunting groups. This is similar to establishing the rules of football or hockey based on the ideas of people who have never experienced the game, have little understanding of it, and think the sport should be banned because of the perceived risk of injury or cruelty in participation. Cultures that cannot even agree on the status of cats, bullfighting, or kosher killing are unlikely to ever reach agreement on the ethics of hunting. To turn ethics legislation on hunting over to politicians is both impractical and unworkable in my opinion.

The antihunting group lobbies for regulations based on ethics because they feel that once a law is passed on this principle, the gate will be opened that leads to the end of hunting, one step at a time. This is the nature of law development in this country. The cancellation of the spring bear hunt was based on an ethical question and touted by extremists as being the first step in the curtailment of hunting. I will discuss this in more detail in the next chapter. It is taking much effort and enormous expense by hunters and their organizations to stem this tide.

One could argue that many of the current hunting regulations are based on ethics, such as not shooting a duck in the water. But in reality, the current laws are based on wildlife conservation principles—the protection, use, and management to sustain the resource at optimum levels and fairly distributed opportunities. This is accomplished by bag limits, seasons, and rules that decrease efficiency, thereby lowering the number harvested when advisable. Some examples are the closed moose season during the rut; the use of bows and arrows, black powder, or shotguns only at given times or in areas for a given species; the outlawing of spotting from airplanes. These regulations are developed cooperatively with specialists in the government and hunting and fishing organizations.

We are fortunate in North America, particularly in Canada, to have such vast areas of wilderness or semiwilderness land. It is a natural resource in which habitat can be cultivated that will sustain hunting and fishing.

Civilization and the ego of modern man have resulted in much thoughtless destruction to Mother Earth and all her creatures. Many in society exaggerate the role hunters play in depleting wildlife and perpetuate the myths associated with hunting. Thoughtful hunters and their organizations have evolved and have changed tremendously for the better. Hunters are obviously more informed about all things to do with hunting, and this translates into continued improvement of ethical behaviour. It is also true that there are thoughtless hunters just as there are thoughtless individuals in other areas of life. It is a challenge on which all of us need to keep working.

CHAPTER 10

On killing

In chapter 8, "More Stories and Psychological Implications," I refer to the reaction of many people to the word "kill" that too often has taken on a very negative connotation, similar to an unholy act. I acknowledge that there are good reasons for this—wars, terrorism, and murders for example.

However, I also point to the other side of the coin—the important and necessary role of killing in the flow of life. Life lives on life, and the reconciliation of this condition is fundamental to accepting hunting.

Joseph Campbell, considered by many as one of the most important thinkers and teachers of this generation, said,

> *Life is, in its very essence and character, a terrible mystery—the whole business of living by killing and eating. But it is a childish attitude to say no to life with all its pain, to say that this is something that should not have been.*

* * *

Killing is an integral element in the balance of nature. Without this balance, many species would increase to a point that they would essentially eliminate all other living matter and eventually themselves.

Some of my friends deride me about my hunting habit because of the killing involved but show negligible concern for animals that die due to encroachment of cities and the subsequent destruction of hundreds of acres a month of habitat. They neither consider the impact of their contribution to this state of affairs by the building of luxurious houses and cottages and through their use of motor vehicles and powered boats. I don't want to appear to be judgemental about anyone's choice of lifestyle, but I find their criticism somewhat ironical in view of the claims of experts who tell us that our consuming lifestyle is by far the greatest destroyer of wildlife and the environment. It is a lifestyle that is depleting and polluting world resources at an alarming rate. On the other hand, the harvesting of a moose or two by me and my party of hunters is designed to sustain the herd.

The harvesting of wildlife is an integral part of conservation. In many areas, there is an overabundance of wildlife. This is damaging great swaths of habitat and depleting food supply to the point where animals are starving. There is more wildlife in North America now than at the early 1900s. In my introduction, I present data that shows that the black bear population has more than doubled since 1966; that the deer population in Ontario has quadrupled in the past few years; that moose numbers have increased; and that there has been an explosive increase in Canada's geese, ducks, and beaver. Deer are destroying farmers' crops and causing motor vehicle accidents. In some areas, the overpopulation is endangering trees, crops, plants, and all of the other life-forms that they support in addition to other animals. Beavers are destroying trees and are becoming a serious health hazard. There is the proliferation of geese that is polluting the parks and beaches of many cities.

Many individuals say that it is fine to kill domestic animals for eating but not beautiful wild animals. They look at me with disbelief when I tell them several of my relatives could not take the life of an animal they had raised for food but could hunt and dress a wild animal. I am greeted with similar disbelief when I say hunters are a positive influence in sustaining wildlife or claim the animals we hunt are treated more humanely than domestic animals raised and slaughtered for food.

Many vegetarians are antihunting mainly in their belief that it is both cruel and unnecessary to kill animals for food. In response to their position, I quote Joseph Campbell, "None of us would be here if we weren't forever eating. What you eat is always something that just a moment before was alive." Dr. Randall Eaton expressed the same thought more bluntly when he wrote, "Vegetarians are just eating something that cannot run away." Campbell and Eaton, as well as other great thinkers, suggest that if God created everything, then everything is an extension of Him and that the robin pulling worms from the garden is naught but God eating himself. Gary Zukov said, "Only when we see through eyes that lack reverence does the feeding of one animal on another appear to be a cruel system instead of one where there is a natural give and take and sharing of energies. This is ecology." Vegetarians choose not to eat meat and are entitled to that choice. But do they have sufficient grounds for asserting judgement, as so many do, or for justifying imposing restrictions on people who raise animals for food or who hunt?

*　　*　　*

The cancellation of the spring bear hunt just prior to an Ontario election illustrates some fallacious thinking about killing. The reason for cancellation of Ontario's spring bear hunt centred on the ethics of killing a mother bear and orphaning her cubs. For some people, "baiting" a hungry mother exacerbated their concern. And while the argument played well in the press, naturalists were quick to point out that it is not only illegal to shoot a mother bear with cubs, but that it was extremely rare for a mother bear with cubs to come to the hunter's bait.

They explained that the mother's instincts and wiles are largely spent on avoiding any perceived dangers including male bears. (Male bears will fight mother bears and devour her young for food. Another reason male bears kill cubs is to eliminate the possibility of future competition.)

Hunters and male bears aside, the birthing experience leaves many mother bears weakened and incapable of feeding their young to a point where as many as 50 percent of bear cubs die of starvation shortly after birth.

It is legal to shoot any bear that is threatening humans or acting in a destructive manner such as harassing and killing farm animals or bees. Otherwise, as already stated, it has been illegal for many years to shoot a female with cubs; and in all this time, only one charge has been laid.

In an imperfect world, more than one such illegal act has probably occurred. But to cancel the spring bear hunt because of some illegal hunting acts makes as much sense as to close the highways on the weekend because of traffic infractions by automobile drivers on their way to the cottage.

And consider this. Due to factors other than hunters, only about 10 percent of cubs survive to breeding age. Without the spring harvest of males (about five thousand per year out of a population of about one hundred thousand in Ontario), the increased number of males contribute significantly to an increase in the killing of cubs. Even more die as roadkill and other causes—the estimate in 2002 was two thousand per year. In other words, cancelling the spring bear hunt to save a few cubs from harm due to possible illegal acts, hundreds die at the hands of nature, and all the benefits of the spring hunt are lost. We should not overlook the fact that bears are predators and added numbers of them will kill more animals of all kinds. For example moose calves, domestic calves, fawns, and sheep are easy pickings for bears.

It is interesting that there is often more concern expressed over the loss of bear cubs than there is for the jobs and other benefits that humans derive from spring bear hunting such as needed bear control, huge revenues, and the benefits of a healthy recreation. A couple of added bonuses from the spring bear hunt were recently mentioned to me by government biologists: (a) most spring bear hunters came from United States and other countries, which aided our foreign exchange; (b) most spring hunters use "baiting" to attract a bear into an open area for a relatively easy shot, less risk of wounding, and a quicker, cleaner kill.

In addition to flawed thinking about killing cubs, I think there is another important consideration, and that is the method used to achieve the cancellation. It illustrates a characteristic of our democratic system and elected representatives—a caution if you will, a weakness some say. Several journalists and others have documented the way it happened. A group of animal rights activists, headed by the wealthy bear-loving industrialist, threatened to run a million-dollar crusade against the incumbents in several crucial ridings during an election campaign unless the spring bear hunt was cancelled. Pathetic video shots of lonely, orphaned cubs were publicized to gain sympathy from tenderhearted Ontario Southerners, most of whom had never seen a bear outside a zoo. The government caved in against the recommendation of experts in their ministry. The party leaders knew the cancellation would garner votes from the large urban population who have an unrealistic perspective about animals. Today, the number of nuisance bears is increasing. They are becoming bolder. More are entering towns and farm areas—harassing people; damaging crops, young trees, property, beehives; killing farmers' livestock and other wilderness animals.

It is regrettable that those most impacted (i.e., those in the northern rural areas) and the people most knowledgeable about the subject were, and are, essentially disregarded in the final decisions made by politicians in faraway Toronto. The decisions will stand unless people in the urban centres become better informed. Wouldn't it be wonderful if we had leaders who were interested in and capable of the teaching required? Is it asking too much? Perhaps this situation supports the pundits who say our

political system is due for reform and that we need to attract a new breed
of politicians.

*   *   *

I had another experience in my early teens that caused me to further
ponder killing. It involved a dog named Trixie. She was a beautiful farm
dog and pet who had mothered many pups. She was also a skilled slayer
of groundhogs and saved the garden and fields from these destructive
pests. One day, my grandmother informed me that Trixie was very sick
and feeble. Grandmother wanted an end to Trixie's suffering, so she asked
if I would put her away.

Of all the people, I wondered, *why me?* Of course, it was because of
my hunting experience. I felt very grown-up at being asked. How best to
accomplish the task was a question in my mind. I learned that the town
policeman exterminated stray dogs by using the exhaust from a fire truck.
I was told that it was a painless method—the dog just fell asleep. So I
decided this was the process I would use. I went to the farm to get Trixie.
She was lying limp but raised her head and weakly wagged her tail in
recognition. I gently lifted her and carried her home in my arms. I then
made her comfortable on a blanket in a cardboard box with a hole in it to
fit over the exhaust pipe. I slipped the box gently into position and started
the car. Trixie began to cry. I couldn't stand it, ran into the house, grabbed
my gun, and put a bullet into her head. She peacefully closed her eyes.

I told Grandma how serenely Trixie had gone. She was very grateful and
complimented me by saying that many people did not have the courage that
I demonstrated, therefore too often avoid doing what needed to be done.

*   *   *

Farm children often adopt a farm animal as a pet and then play with it as
it grows up. It is a natural tendency when one helps in the birth of a lamb,
calf, or piglet. Sooner or later, the animal has to be killed for food, a traumatic
experience for a child; and many farmers take great pains to explain to
their children the reasons for not becoming too fond of the farm animals.

The 4-H club has an interesting program for developing responsibility
in youths and providing a proper perspective on killing. In this program, a
youth is assigned the responsibility to care for a calf from the moment of
birth until it is sent off to a slaughter for food. The youth gives the newborn

a name, essentially adopts it as a pet, and takes care of its every need including cleaning the stall, feeding, grooming, exercising, and training it so that it will show well at a contest. The day after the judging contest, the youth's "pet" is taken away to serve its role in the food chain. In this way, the youth has been taught a valuable lesson about life.

Contrast this with people who tell their children to love and treat all living things as they would their pet dog and then teach them about the cruelty they perceive in the processing of animals for food.

To love animals is natural, and there are numerous benefits to having a pet. But there is also a reality that needs be honoured and understood.

Young people who have been taught the realities of the food chain usually accept hunting as a personal choice. Those that haven't too often provide the platform that cultivates extremists who try to force their beliefs on others.

I agree with those who say it is very important that children learn the realities of life in order to effectively cope with the workings of the world—that this is a prerequisite to achieving happiness and health. Knowledge and understanding is something that cannot be poured into the brain—it requires the active engagement of the individual.

Perceived cruelty in the methods used in the killing of animals is a common objection to the sport of hunting. I sometimes ask, what method would a person consider not cruel? I rarely get a straight answer. The person often states they do not approve of this or that method and reiterates that they do not believe in cruelty to animals and that there must be a better way. I have struggled with this question many times myself, for instance, in the case of Trixie mentioned above.

Over the years, I have tried and witnessed several methods—shooting; clubbing the head; a special knife piercing the heart, brain, or throat; drowning; suffocation by snare or trap; poisoning with chemical mixed with food; poisonous gas; and injections. My grandmother had a special knifelike tool she preferred for preparing her chickens for the dinner table. My aunt chopped their heads off and didn't seem to mind the chicken flailing or running headless around the yard. I once met a government agent who was sent to teach farmers the right way to prepare animals for food. He used a sledgehammer to the head, but after witnessing this, my uncle still preferred to shoot his animals. In the case of small creatures, I have found a sharp blow to their head causes the least reaction by the animal—even less than a veterinarian's needle delivering a fatal drug. There probably is no way that would meet with the approval of everyone—interpretation is essentially "in the eye of the beholder."

CHAPTER 11

Trends of concern

*What is dangerous about extremists is not that they are extreme,
but that they are intolerant. The evil is not that what they say
about their cause, but what they say about their opponents.*
—Robert Kennedy

Let me address some specific trends that discourage hunting. I find these especially pertinent because many of my acquaintances suggest I am overreacting to a few radicals. Overreacting, perhaps, but consider the following:

*It is violence against the innocent. It's killing for the hell of it.
It's rather like child-molesting.*
—Governor General Award—winner John Livingston

Hunters are nothing more than recreational killers.
—Ontario government lawyers
defending cancellation of the spring bear hunt

Get the damn hunter's guns out of Toronto.
—Mel Lastman, mayor of Toronto

David Miller, who followed Mel Lastman as mayor, has been on television and in the newspapers repeatedly in his thrust to have guns banned. He states, "A person in possession of a gun will eventually use it." (His implication being that the gun would be used in a criminal act.)

I came to Ottawa with the firm belief that the only people in this country who should have guns are police officers and soldiers.
                                        —Allan Rock, justice minister

This could be the start of a global movement that would spur development of an instrument to ban firearms worldwide similar to our land mines initiative.
                                        —Herb Gray, deputy prime minister of
                            Canada supporting words for Bill C68/ Firearms Act

The foregoing declarations are infiltrating the thinking of many. They often say that the only purpose of a gun is to kill. One example of the outcome of this thinking is the program Operation Gun Play—No Way mandated in 2002 by Toronto's chief of police at the request of some concerned parents and politicians. Centres were set up across the city and manned by police officers. Four- to fourteen-year-old children were encouraged to come to these centres where they were informed that toy guns and playing with them were bad. If kids turned in their toy guns, they were given a doll, a book, or a bag of candies. The premise cited for the program was that this would reduce their misuse of real guns in later life.

I suggest we work at keeping things in perspective. There is ample evidence that misuse of motor vehicles by criminals and others is a significant problem. In reality, motor vehicle misuse causes thousands of times more problems than firearms do; and licensing and registration has done little, if anything, to change this. Would it make sense to take away toy motor vehicles from children and teach them that they are bad? If such an approach decreases the misuse of guns, why wouldn't the same logic apply for motor vehicle misuse?

What a ridiculous idea most say, pointing out that motor vehicles are not the same as guns and that, in our society, cars are a necessity though many would admit that motor vehicles are used to excess. The point I want to make is that both items are tools or weapons that can be used for good or bad, depending on the person. This was vividly illustrated by the disaster of 9/11 where airplanes were used as a destructive tool to destroy skyscrapers and kill thousands.

Another point to consider in the case of Operation Gun Play is the use of valuable police time. It seems to me that it would more effectively be employed chasing criminals rather than telling kids that toy guns are bad. When I suggested this to police officers and several parents, some agreed while others responded that there are some toy guns with which a child can hurt himself and that this was their main concern. There are many things with which kids can hurt themselves—including other toys (bicycles, skateboards, knives) and a host of household items. Why single out toy guns? Could it be a subconscious fear?—a condition known to cause flawed thinking.

It is not my purpose to demean the supporters of such programs. The point I am attempting to emphasize is that sometimes we can benefit from a more reasoned approach and that priorities need to be considered when using limited, valuable resources.

Perhaps counsel about the nature of the law of attraction by men such as Plato, Hugo, Shakespeare, Einstein, Lincoln, Emerson, to name a few, warrants greater consideration. This law states that we attract into our life whatever dominates our thoughts and emotions. Positive emotions and thoughts attract positive results; negative emotions and thoughts attract negative results. The placebo effect illustrates this concept. You may have noticed that people who complain a lot get more to complain about.

> *Beware what you set your heart upon. For it shall surely be yours.*
> —Ralph Waldo Emerson

> *It is a universal law that what we fear will come to us. As strange as it may seem, we create the reality we fear. Fearful thoughts create fearful consequences. Poison thoughts create a poison world.*
> —Dr. Randall Eaton

I find it ironic that the reason given for cancelling the toy gun program was that too many kids were buying a toy pistol at a dollar store and turning it in for a more valuable doll, book, or candy.

Here is another perception held by many people that deserves analysis: "The only purpose of a gun is to kill." The predominate thought for this statement is that all killing is bad and that ownership of guns is bad. Refer to chapter 10, "On Killing," which discusses many worthy aspects of "killing." The purpose of a police and security officer's gun is not to kill. They primarily are used as a deterrent to criminals. Let's not overlook that firearms are used in many sports activities from which children and adults learn safety, responsibility, and self-worth. The Olympic Games recognize some of these.

There is plenty of evidence that while current attempts to demonize guns have resulted in many gun laws, those laws have done little, if anything, towards steering us towards a happier, safer society. For example, Toronto's chief of police has been quoted saying that in all his years of policing, he has never experienced so much violence with guns. I think most observers would agree with his assessment. There were 378 more calls involving guns in 2003 over 2002 (August 6, 2003, in the *Globe and Mail*). A further increase in crime involving guns occurred in Toronto in 2005. It is interesting to note that during this same period, crime was reduced dramatically in New York and Boston without the type of strict gun control laws implemented in Canada. But despite evidence that many of our gun controls are not producing the intended results, there is a continuing cry for more and stricter controls. By contrast, little has been suggested to tackle the real problem with vigour—the people behind the guns. (This subject is discussed in detail in chapter 13, "Firearms and Crime," and in chapter 14, "The Firearms Registry System and Implications.") Perhaps all the reports in the news media about guns and statements that often smack of fearmongering by politicians are actually creating excessive fear in people.

*   *   *

Focusing on the "evil" product not only misses the target but also discourages useful activities and experiences that come with constructive use of the instrument. Concentrating on the product diverts us from the seed of the problem and from applying the resources to effectively address prevention. I suggest we could better tackle these problems by planting and cultivating family values, a reverence for life, a strong work ethic, and a sense of personal responsibility for constructively handling difficulties and to instil this in children at a very early age. We should not, I suggest, be using hardship as an excuse for improper behaviour. Severe penalties for misuse are helpful, but don't get to the heart of the problem.

*   *   *

One side effect of promoting the fear of guns is that it discourages hunting. If guns are bad, then hunting must be bad.

A study was published in 2002 by Gary Mauser, a professor of business administration at the University of British Columbia and an internationally recognized expert on crime who has written over thirty publications on the subject. "Many gun owners are abandoning hunting or owning firearms in the face of the increasing arbitrariness of firearm legislation," writes Mauser. "Parents are finding it increasingly difficult to pass on the values of their rural hunting culture to the next generation."

Mauser also pointed out, "In all cases, the effort (firearms legislation) meant setting up expensive bureaucracies that produced no noticeable improvement to public safety or have made the situation worse."

*   *   *

Other legislation that affects hunting is also a concern. For example, the new bill that has been passed by our federal House of Commons makes cruelty to animals a criminal offence. Fortunately, it has been stalled in the Senate for revisions (2006). In general, the intention is good—we all agree that undue cruelty to animals should not be tolerated. The problem is in the definition of "animal," "pain," and "cruelty." In the bill, an animal is defined as "any creature that has a vertebra or feels pain." However, "pain" is an awfully generic term. Some feel that suffocation is such a painful and cruel way to die that sportfishing should be stopped; others feel that the method for killing an animal suitable for kosher food is cruel. For many people, the squirming of a frog or worm as it is placed on a fishhook is too cruel to bear. People from countries where the cow is sacred have special considerations related to that animal. A retired professor of philosophy recently explained to me that he really had nothing against hunting but thought sportfishing should be stopped because suffocation was such a horribly cruel way to die. The slogan by animal rights activists against sportfishing says, "How would you like to die of suffocation? This is how a fish dies." Their literature is showing up in a growing number of schools. People for Ethical Treatment of Animals (PETA) has a Web site devoted to the idea that hooking a fish in the lips is similar to hooking a human in the lips. The list is extensive. I wonder if there is an acceptable way to kill an octopus or lobster.

How pain is to be determined is a knotty question. Certainly, all creatures feel something that makes them struggle for survival and may look like pain. But to put this in the same category as human pain and call it "cruel" is not realistic or supported by scientific evidence. Even so, the foregoing bill will open the door for many challenges in the courts. For instance, animal rights activists claim that the proposed law is an important step in their agenda to stop sports hunting. The fact that the majority of our elected representatives (federal House of Commons) passed the bill three times after extensive debate has all the elements of succumbing to popular notions and the politics of party power.

The thought of harming the cute baby animals portrayed in videos and photos tugs at the hearts of most. The videos produced by animal rights activists are created to shock us with the bloody mess that occurs in the taking of an animal's life. It is not a pretty picture and creates flawed conclusions in many people. Squeamishness about taking the life of an animal in the field or in a slaughterhouse is exacerbated by city life. An extensive survey of youths in 2003 by an organization (Responsive Management) reveals interesting phenomena. They reported that a majority of boys did not want to hunt because they did not want to kill animals, and yet only 5 percent of them were vegetarians.

Maybe we would be better served by viewing nature in a more enlightened way. I believe if we take a close look at all the evidence, we can observe that nature has marvellously adaptive ways to handle what some see as suffering and cruelty. For example, my sons were taught in school that aboriginals are cruel to their dogs because they leave them out in the cold. In reality, a healthier sled dog develops when he is kept in the cold.

I suggest that this ability to adapt is a quality that has, unfortunately, been allowed to atrophy in humans. I think that some of the energy used anguishing over certain aspects of pain would be better directed at finding ways to improve our natural pain-reducing capabilities. Modern individuals, too often, make their own pain worse than it needs be. For example, training in natural childbirth and pain management in recent years has allowed many mothers to experience childbirth without strong painkillers or anaesthetics. This has health benefits for both mother and baby. Pain-management training has also helped many chronic-pain sufferers by enabling them to reduce (sometimes discontinue) the use of painkilling drugs. I realize this is a complex subject that needs more exploration than given here. However, it is a condition that I became aware of partly due to my hunting experience. There is ample evidence in many books that man's mind influences his feelings and his body, both positively and negatively. From this perspective, there are many conditions in life that would be easier to endure with an appropriate frame of mind.

*   *   *

One of the positions of the antihunting and conservation lobbies is that any overpopulation problems with wild creatures can best be solved by nature, that nature naturally finds a balance, that this method was effective before man came. "Have faith in the natural process," they say. I wonder if they feel the same way about mice, rats, flies, and bacteria that infest foods. Should we stop fighting all forest fires and go back to wearing just a loincloth? Of course not—realistically, it is not possible to turn back the clock; and like it or not, man is now part of the equation, part of nature, and part of the "natural process."

Perhaps the time has come for an emerging awareness of the interconnectivity of all things and a greater dedication of man's resources to develop more ways to improve his role in assisting nature. For example, a search on the Web shows that in 2004, worldwide military spending topped $1 trillion in the name of security. Imagine what this kind of expenditure, or even 10 percent of it, could do to help Mother Nature.

*   *   *

In this rapidly changing world, issues are becoming increasingly complex, and we do not have the time to become knowledgeable in all subjects. Worldwide and instantaneous communications flood us with information. People, in their enthusiasm for their causes, spread information that is frequently misleading. What looks at first blush like a good idea often begins to unravel on closer examination.

Because of the complexities, we elect representatives to governments, expecting them to become experts and trusting them to make good decisions on policy and then lead us in understanding the route that best serves society.

But the democratic process is susceptible to some undesirable pressures. For instance, it is easy for politicians to fall into the trap of developing policies based on polls and pressure groups—the politics of focus groups over the politics of evidence and fact. Rather than clarifying issues, politicians often fan the flames by exaggerating concerns and then offer simple, quick solutions. They do this because it is an effective way of winning votes—their primary motivation is self-serving, personal power. It is an approach that frequently results in inappropriate laws that are Band-Aid treatments at best or in the long term do harm. This is precisely what has happened with laws that negatively impact hunting. Events related in following sections will highlight this unfortunate state of affairs.

Many political pundits claim we are overdue for an overhaul of governing processes, leadership skills training, and ethics. They are calling for a reinvigoration of proper democratic processes, a more cooperative spirit with less strict adherence to party line. They suggest we would be better served by finding a way to tackle problems without demonizing different ideas and the people who propose them—an approach that is more likely to foster improved solutions. According to the pundits, current governing has degenerated into what they refer to as political posturing, which essentially means establishing policy based on opinion polls. They point out that good-quality leaders would use opinion polls primarily as indicators to determine where voters might need more information to guide them to a better understanding. Such leaders would hone their investigative and evidence-gathering methods as well as their ability as educators and would not succumb easily to opinion polls. To highlight this, Winston Churchill is often quoted with his cautioning statement, "The greatest argument against democracy is a five-minute conversation with the average voter." Many great leaders have made similar statements. I recently listened to excerpts from Churchill's speeches, presented to illustrate his insightful grasp of situations and his tremendous ability to change perceptions, even inspire people, with educational evidence presented eloquently. Churchill was often punished at the polls for sticking to his assessment of situations—for example, the position he took on the dangers of Hitler, well in advance of public opinion. He is now accepted as one of the great statesmen in history. I think most people at this time agree that improved approaches and measuring systems are very much needed for our government(s)—methods that hold elected representatives more accountable and motivate them, hopefully inspire them, to serve society better. I am sure that such changes would lead to different approaches to several of the thrusts that have a negative impact on hunting as well as other government actions that are too often too simplistic and poll driven to be effective.

CHAPTER 12

Perceived dangers in hunting

Many people believe that hunting is extremely dangerous. A survey of youths by a group called Responsive Management found that the majority of participants perceived hunting as a dangerous sport. Many people are discouraged from hunting because of the perceived danger. I recently played golf with a retired executive of a large company who told me that he refused to hunt after reading a newspaper report that during hunting season, there were as many hunters shot as deer—which is a horrible manipulation of data.

There were, in fact, only four accidents and no deaths involved with the 423,000 hunters in Ontario in 2001. This surely speaks well for the training devoted to firearms and hunting safety. By contrast, almost a quarter-million Canadians are hurt or killed each year in a motor vehicle. In Ontario alone, the latest data published, at the time of this writing, by the Ontario government (2001) show that there were 437,410 car accidents.

Mandatory hunter-safety training has made hunting one of the safest outdoor activities. I pointed out in chapter 3, "Benefits of Hunting," that Dr. Terry Quinney in his research found hunting to be safer than golf, horseback riding, bicycling, baseball, and swimming. Lightning is twenty times the danger, and the automobile, eighteen thousand times.

We frequently witness overreaction to data that gets attention due to interest groups, an incident, or study. Every day in the news, we see and hear something to worry us if we let it or have preconceived concerns on the topic. You don't want to know how many people die each year while swimming; otherwise, you might never go near the water again.

Certainly, hunting can be dangerous; and occasionally, there are accidents. Firearms, like other all equipment, need to be handled carefully.

Everything we do entails risk that can only be reduced through personal responsibility. Do not tailgate while travelling one hundred kilometres per hour. Don't golf in a thunderstorm. Don't mow your lawn in your bare feet. Do not stumble about in the woods with the safety off on your rifle and your finger on the trigger.

It is sometimes tough to put things in perspective because of all the hype in the news about "gun crime." In my experience, people who want more restrictions on firearms have significantly less concern for much greater dangers—including their motor vehicles and swimming pools, not to mention their diets. Occasionally, thoughtful journalists point this out. In January 2006, an article in the *Toronto Star* was headlined, IN GTA, CAR IS DEADLIER THAN GUN. The article stated, "We are horrified by 52 gun killings (Greater Toronto Area, 2005, population 5.7 million) but 229 traffic fatalities are accepted as a fact of modern life." That year (2005) was touted as the "year of the gun" because of a spike in killings in Toronto, due mostly to gang wars and drugs. Politicians at all levels duked it out, trying to outdo one another with promises of tougher gun controls using methods that are essentially the same as those already in place and without any evidence of effectiveness. Some have actually made the situation worse (refer to the following chapters for details). Gun control as a means of achieving greater safety was a major issue during the federal election, but nothing was mentioned about the large number of deaths by motor vehicles and the huge number of injuries by motor vehicles. For every fatality by automobiles, there are many, many injuries. My son's crushed skull, which was caused by a drunk driver ramming his car into the vehicle in which my son was a passenger, was as much a concern for me as a wound by a gun would have been. Similarly, my grandfather's leg injury by an intruder's axe was as much a concern as if he had been shot—in fact, a bullet would have done much less damage. If I have the choice of a taking a road where there has been one or two deaths and a couple of injuries by gun or one that has ten deaths and a several hundred injuries by automobiles, I know which I would select as the safest by far. However, I don't give these risks more than passing thought. Perhaps we should be thankful for the odds of fifty-two in 5.7 million. It is an excellent safety record compared with most parts of the world. The risk of death due to heart disease is many times greater depending on one's age.

Nonetheless, the mayor of Toronto and many other politicians at all levels of government continue their rhetoric about shootings and need for more gun controls. This has resulted in many people taking a different position from mine about safety on our streets. For example, at a dinner party I attended, there were guests from another country; and a suggestion was made by friends that the guests refrain from visiting downtown Toronto because of the danger of being shot. These same friends invited the guests to visit their cottage without realizing that the trip on the busy highways exposed them to a much higher risk of death and serious injury in "an automobile accident" (thousands of times higher). From my point of view, worrying about such risk is not healthy or productive. The foregoing attitude about dangers on the streets of Toronto is all too common and unfortunately results in unconstructive and inappropriate actions.

The notion that guns are a worse threat than motor vehicles is primarily because of the preconceived idea that cars are not designed to kill whereas guns are. This lacks sound reasoning if one looks beyond the surface. Many developments originated for war purposes and as an aid "to kill"—axes, knives, radio technology, atomic power, and motorized vehicles to name a few. These developments also spawned or became tools for constructive use. In any case, an argument for or against a product or tool based on original intent is irrelevant. I don't think any of us would want to eliminate knives and axes.

It is human nature to have difficulty in comprehending activities in which we lack experience as well as to side with prevailing notions. We need to be aware of these traits and be sympathetic of those who are unaware of or doubt the beneficial use of guns because they have no experience in such activities. However, we should not accept the intolerance of those who try to force their perception on others. We should try to find a better path to better understanding.

A major reason people are more accepting of death and injury by cars compared with those by guns is because in our society, people are familiar with cars and their many benefits. In many cases, the perception that cars are a necessity is misguided and often misleading. Most deaths and injuries by motor vehicles occur when they are in use for what could be classified as "unnecessary" activities such as convenience or pleasure.

I have observed that the responsibility a person learns through hunting extends into other activities in life. I think you will agree that knowledge gained in one area usually benefits us in others as well. Could we be more adept at convincing people of the advantages of taking part in sports that use firearms and, at the same time, help in clarifying and prioritizing issues? I suggest that hunters work at this because of their knowledge about firearms, hunting, and the negative implications of some popular attitudes and controls.

CHAPTER 13

Firearms and crime

The subject of firearms needs to be addressed for several reasons. We are all concerned about guns and violence, and there are good reasons for such concerns, but understanding reasons does not necessarily bring sensible answers.

> *Fundamentally, a society that asks questions and has the power to answer them is a healthier society than one that simply accepts what is told from a narrow range of experts, institutions, and politicians. We need to be encouraged to think for ourselves.*
> —Chris Anderson in his brilliant
> and timely book *The Long Tail*

Man is distinguished from other predators by his ability to design and use tools. The first tools were sticks and stones. Further developments include the sharp-edged stone that evolved into the knife, spear, and arrow. Explosives led to dynamite and firearms. All tools can be used constructively or destructively. All have provided more good than harm. I don't think we would want to revert to not having them. The tool is inanimate. The decision on how it is used rests with the individual who uses it.

The first recorded act of violence was when Cain slew his brother, Abel, out in the field. The villain was not the club. It was Cain. The heart of the problem is in the heart and mind of man.

Most "gun" problems occur in conjunction with drug or alcohol use. There are many reports that link them. If alcohol and drug problems were eliminated, most gun problems would disappear. I invite you to take a close look at this. Visit any courtroom and witness the number of alcohol, drug, and motor vehicle-related cases. Problems with firearms are miniscule by comparison. A recent study showed that 30 percent of hospital-bed occupants had alcohol-related illnesses. I am not implying we needn't have concerns about guns. However, our resources are limited, which means there is a much need for prioritizing and bringing rational reasoning to optimize results. Also, I think we are overlooking the fact that destructive weapons are as difficult to eliminate as drugs and alcohol, perhaps more difficult. There are many destructive tool alternatives, including an easily fabricated homemade bomb, crossbow, or potato gun. Focusing on the product seldom solves the problems. Tough laws on misuse help, but the solution is even more complex than that. We need to get to the roots of the problem so that focus can be appropriately directed. Education by parents and society in the proper use of products and instilling a sense of personal responsibility in individuals, along with a reverence for life, has had the most success by far.

Perhaps we can learn from prohibition laws in the 1920s that are analogous to the gun laws of Bill C68. Prohibition that demonized alcohol and all imbibers did not cure alcoholism but resulted in increased crime. Programs such as Alcoholics Anonymous that teach people about the dangers of alcohol, the importance of taking personal responsibility, and a reverence for life have had far more success. Severe penalties for criminal behaviour also have their place. Tough love works. Trying to solve misuse by blaming the product is generally not effective, discriminates against the responsible majority, and detracts from benefits that come with constructive use.

Unfortunately, we are witnessing much confused thinking. When a warped mind kills with a gun, our urban society tends to attach blame to the gun. Incidents involving guns get a lot of news coverage and commentary, further fanning the fires of fear.

In the passion that marks the aftermath of tragedies, concerns are understandable. But that doesn't necessarily make the proposed solutions reasonable. Many offered solutions only scratch the surface and divert us away from searching for deeper insights that, in the long term, will provide more effective answers.

No doubt, there are a number of reasons why so many people are not sensible about solutions to problems associated with firearms. Many people who don't own a gun or have had no hands-on experience with them seem to feel that owning a gun invites crime and promotes violence and that possession of several types of guns increases the dangers. Too many people feel guns and violence go hand in hand and that if guns were eliminated, violence would almost disappear. I frequently hear and see the term "gun violence." The news media is not responsible for this as much as viewers are. In my opinion, too many are seeing and hearing only what they want to see or hear. There are also politicians in governments who promote people's fears to suit their self-serving purposes. The dangers of knives, explosives, and a host of other potential weapons are not given the same attention even though some are used more frequently in crime. It is not understood that a hunter has several types of guns for similar reasons that a golfer has several types of golf clubs, each for a specific application. A person does not pose more danger because of the number of guns he owns. In fact, he poses less danger than average because of safety training and a sense of responsibility that comes with hunting and wilderness experiences.

Overlooked is the criminal mind that finds or makes destructive weapons. If one is seized, he will soon find another or will fabricate one. Most people are not aware of how easy this is. I don't mean to imply that there should be no controls, but their effectiveness needs better analysis.

Perceptions are indeed interesting and sometimes misleading. "But your guns are not necessary," argue some friends as we speed down the highway in a big car at 140 kilometres per hour en route to a golf tournament. This weapon is capable of 240 kilometres per hour, and the safety is off. My attempts to point out the similarities to firearms are scoffed at. I am told that cars are necessary while the only purpose for a gun is to kill. The many constructive uses of guns are not recognized such as aboriginal and trapper livelihood, sport shooting, hunting, and other activities in which people find enjoyment and learn. They find it unreasonable to consider that most deaths and injuries by motor vehicles occur during what could be classified as "unnecessary" activities such as convenience or pleasure trips. They resist suggestions that many developments originated for military and "killing" purposes have also spawned other applications such as airplanes, motor vehicles, atomic energy, and guns to name a few of the many products. Another question asked is, why do you need several guns? One friend responds that he can see the similarity to a set of golf clubs where each one has a unique application. Although such discussions create an improved understanding for some, others don't get the point—they have an underlying belief that has permeated much our society: *guns are bad.*

Data gathered by the United States Department of Health and Human Services add an interesting perspective. It shows that accidental death is thousands of times more likely to be caused by a physician than a gun owner. According to the *Journal of the American Medical Association*, medical treatment is the third leading cause of death after heart disease and cancer. I mention this not to create a fear of doctors but to help create a more realistic perspective on gun ownership and thus alleviate the high level of fear displayed of guns.

Previously, I mentioned a study by Gary Mauser who reported, "Many gun owners are abandoning hunting or owning firearms in the face of the increasing arbitrariness of firearm legislation. Parents are finding it increasingly difficult to pass on the values of their rural hunting culture to the next generation."

Mauser also pointed out, "In all cases, the effort (firearms legislation) meant setting up expensive bureaucracies that produce no noticeable improvement to public safety or have made the situation worse."

CHAPTER 14

The firearms registry system and implications

La raison avant la passion (reason over passion).
—Pierre Elliott Trudeau

We all want a safer society and abhor the use of guns in criminal acts. The firearms registry was created in an attempt to address this concern soon after a terrible tragedy in Montreal where a deranged student murdered fourteen women. It was a political expedient that at first appeared to be a step in the right direction.

As comforting as the registry may seem to many nongun owners, proof is lacking that registration has made society safer in its eight years of operation. Since 1998, all firearms are required to be registered.

The firearms registry is a major concern for Canadians. It imposes a very high cost in terms of money and manpower. It also discourages law-abiding people from gun ownership but not criminals. Many people have been led to feel guns are bad. Yet guns are a basic component in hunting. Therefore, the gun registry has had an insidious effect that tends to squeeze the life out of hunting. This is one of the concerns of hunters and anyone who is aware of the many benefits of hunting. An even greater concern is the philosophy that drives the registry—every time a crime is committed using a gun, there is a hue and cry for more gun control using methods with no proof of effectiveness.

We often hear from some leaders in the house of Parliament and in debates and interviews addressing opponents of the long gun registry, "Why do you not want to do everything possible to help police?"

"We register cars. Why not guns?" There's no quick, easy answer.

Canada is not the only country struggling with this problem. Both Australia and the United Kingdom introduced gun registries and other such laws. But despite the effort, police statistics show that the United Kingdom is experiencing a serious crime wave, and Australia's homicide rate remained flat from 1995 to 2001. In Australia, the destruction of confiscated firearms cost taxpayers the equivalent of C$420 million with no visible impact on violent crime. (The cost of the confiscation does not include the costs of bureaucracy, which is considerable.)

In Canada, since firearms were required to be registered (1998), the homicide rate has increased by more than 3 percent. The percent of homicides with guns has remained the same at 27 percent. The percentage of family homicides involving firearms has remained at 23 percent. While homicides involving guns are down from the peak in the 1970s, the total homicide rate has increased. This indicates that crime rates are driven by sociological factors rather than availability of just one method for murder. The bottom line is the registry has not saved any lives or created a safer society.

Would a firearm ban be effective? In the 1970s, both the Republic of Ireland and Jamaica passed legislation to prohibit all firearms. Neither country has the attempt to ban, nor confiscation of firearms reduced the homicide rate. In Canada, weapons that have been prohibited—such as fully automatic firearms, short barrel handguns, and knives with a push button for opening—often show up in the hands of criminals.

In fact, it needs to be asked if the money spent on stringent gun laws might be better spent on other programs. Make no mistake, gun laws impose a very high cost on citizens by stimulating the growth of government bureaucracy and through compensation for confiscating banned weapons.

I am not suggesting that some good isn't derived through gun registration and that some criminals may have been apprehended using it. But a more important consideration should be, Is it an effective way to spend our limited resources? An increasing number of articles are being written stating that the money spent on the registry is money that could be more wisely put to better use; therefore, the registry will indirectly cost more lives than it will ever save.

An article in the *Ottawa Citizen* (September 2002) pointed out that the $1 billion registry costs could be used much more effectively to purchase magnetic resonance imaging equipment (MRIs) and other diagnostic equipment.

My intention is not to blame but to inform. For sure, we can't improve something that we do not recognize.

Maybe public policy changes left too many ill people and violent criminals on Canadian streets. Perhaps we would be better off investing money spent on the gun registry in better detection and treatment of the mentally ill. I suggest there are many areas in which we are being too lenient or not providing effective guidance.

When Canada's gun registry was proposed, it was claimed that it would cost $85 million, but the auditor general found that the costs of only part of the registry were more than $1 billion. And she did not examine the entire sprawling program. Estimates of the total cost now exceed $2 billion.

I think we would be wise to take a careful look at the entire scene, including the "political-posturing" and "fearmongering" culture that has developed, clearly demonstrated by the gun registry issue. There are several reasons for concern that are indicated by the firearms scenario, which I will attempt to clarify.

The supporters keep bringing forth data that they seem to think supports the registry. Here are a few examples: The number of firearms applications rejected and firearms destroyed is extensively publicized by the news media and various agencies. To think that telling a criminal he can't have a gun stops him from obtaining one or making a homemade weapon or committing a crime is wishful thinking. And so is the idea of scrapping guns. Too often, the rationale appears to be that everything that can be counted counts.

Would scrapping knives, baseball bats, or any one of many other tools reduce crime? Of course it wouldn't. Although there are cases which may be worthwhile, they are few and far between and don't come close to justifying the huge costs.

The literature that claims gun registration promotes safe storage and handling of firearms is more blarney. Does registering cars promote safe storage and handling of cars? (Every thirteen minutes, a car is stolen in Canada.) Less costly and less intrusive methods have a confirmed improvement record.

The police chiefs who want the system quote the number of queries on the system as "justification for the system." I am sure it is nice to know information, perhaps some good gleaned; but in terms of creating a safer society, there is scant meaningful evidence.

The promoters of firearms registration tout the number of suicides using a gun as an example that they feel justifies discouraging firearm ownership. I know several people who will not allow a gun in their homes for this reason. On March 15, 2001, an article in the *Toronto Star* reported that in Britain, "For their own protection, farmers have had their guns taken from them by the police." The reason given was a fear that they might commit suicide over their cattle problems. Based on my investigations, I agree with the majority of experts on suicide—there is no sustainable evidence that suicide rate is influenced by gun ownership. It may be the tool of preference in some cultures; however, where there is the will, there will always be a way.

As much as we all wish for a society free of guns for crime, in reality, registering all firearms is not doing the job. Even banning them has not been successful. Illegal (banned) firearms are commonly used in crime. The reality is that those with criminal intent can acquire an illegal gun in many ways. Seventy years of trying has not stopped illegal trafficking in guns. Even if that avenue was closed entirely, the homemade potato gun, blowgun, or bomb would quickly show up, fabricated from readily available material and "how to" instructions accessible on the Internet. Look what happened in Oklahoma City on April 19, 1995. Tim McVeigh, an oddball loner, blew up a building with a homemade bomb made with fertilizer and other readily available ingredients. Over 160 people were killed, and many more injured. And then there is the 9/11 example.

I am not advocating zero gun control, but as the auditor general and others have suggested, let's make sure that what we are doing is an effective way of spending our limited supply of money and law enforcement resources. A greater awareness of this state of affairs would point us in a preferable direction, in my opinion.

There are many ways to kill: knives, poison, baseball bats, hammers, machetes, cars, airplanes, dynamite, bombs for instance. How effective would it be to limit the use of any or all of these tools if we want to reduce murder? The answer, quite simply, is that it would not be effective at all.

There is a movement afoot that advocates we would be a healthier and wealthier society by doing more to teach people basic responsibility and emphasizing the important role of parents, religious leaders, and others in the process. Children need to learn the values that include a respect for life and not feeling sorry for themselves. They need to learn that hardship is not an excuse for improper behaviour and that everyone has a responsibility to develop themselves constructively and to do the proper things. There are jurisdictions, Boston and New York for example, where this approach has had far more success in reducing crime and criminal use of guns than has firearms registration. I think this is another illustration of the universal law of attraction mentioned in chapter 11, "Trends of Concern." The universe delivers to us where we focus our thoughts and emotions. To benefit by this law, we need to be clear on our goals. We should strive to create a safe society and concentrate on creating good people, which tends to attract more good people. Concentrating on the evil gun, on the other hand, tends to attract more misuse of guns. Fearful thoughts produce fearful results; it's as simple as that. Unfortunately, we tend to focus on what we don't want rather than focusing on what we want. This realization lies behind the remarks made by Mother Theresa: "People ask me why I don't join the antiwar movement, and I say, 'I will join when you show me a propeace movement.'"

My intense interest in the firearms registry system, which includes its policy/procedures, is partly due to my hunting interest.

Most firearms owners find the firearms registry system to be complex, bureaucratic, and intrusive. In chapter 11, "Trends of Concern," I quote from a study by Gary Mauser. He found that many gun owners are abandoning hunting or owning firearms and that parents are finding it increasingly difficult to pass on the values of their hunting culture in the face of the increasing arbitrariness of firearm legislation. The difficulties the system poses deter many people from participating in healthy sports activities from which children and adults learn safety, responsibility, and self-worth.

Most nongun owners tend to be insensitive to the complications the registry system imposes on hunters and other legitimate firearms users. Moreover, they are apathetic or don't seem to recognize the propaganda and viewpoint behind the registration system that is pushing for even more restrictions.

Registration per se is not the main issue. The concern is about all of the foregoing, the thinking that gave birth to the system and perpetrated by its administration policies. Supporters of the registry continue to demand even further restrictions on firearms. The methods proposed, similar to those of the registry, will yield similarly unsatisfactory results and impose even more problems for those who want to participate in those healthy activities in which guns are used. The demands intensify with every gun crime in the country.

*   *   *

The development of the system is an interesting study into political processes. The intentions that gave us the system are wonderful, but the issue is complex, and the results disappointing, to say the least.

As my mother used to say, "The road to hell is paved with good intentions." Looking beyond the surface of things is important.

Several political pundits and others have suggested that the politicians who promoted the registry were primarily using the terrible tragedy in Montreal where a deranged student murdered fourteen women. Certainly, the public was anxious and willing to support politicians who promised to do something that would prevent such occurrences from ever happening again. The passion that marks the aftermath of such tragedies is understandable. However, a large majority of people didn't have and still don't have the experience or time to make the proper in-depth evaluation.

The auditor general requested that evidence be produced to show existing gun control laws were effective, or not, in reducing crime before proceeding with the expensive registry system. This was not done. Information from many experts that showed the system would not achieve the promised results and would cost far more than the government estimate was ignored—and the messengers ridiculed.

Initially, I supported the idea of a registry as a method to help police. But as details of Bill C68 unfolded—the policies, objectives, and type of system proposed—I recognized that many of the objectives would not be met and that society could realize far more benefits by applying the money and resources to areas other than the expensive registry. There are simpler ways to achieve many of the desired results. My experience in the computer field made me aware that many people too often view computers as a panacea, only to be disappointed after spending millions of dollars. I also had unique knowledge gained from experience with on-line, real-time computer systems for controlling costly computer parts, down to items in kits carried by service personnel across the country. I understood the complexities, the tremendous costs involved, and inventory inaccuracies inherent in such an environment. I was also aware that most inventory experts had difficulty understanding this unique environment. My association with members of the police force also helped me to see flaws in the thinking about the system's ability to satisfy the stated goals and wishes. The politicians promised much more than could reasonably be delivered. Too many policemen accepted the promises as did the public. I became aware that the registration system would not be a cost-effective means of crime prevention and control nor would it prevent the illegal use of guns. I asked several policemen if 70 percent accuracy in the inventory of firearms would be tolerable for police work. An emphatic no was the unanimous reply. Guess what? One of the major complaints after a few years of operation is errors and inaccuracies in the database. Just a short time ago, major problems with security of information in the system were reported—a shocking problem in such a system and one that is very costly to fix. Bill C68 is one of those nifty policies that fall apart under close study.

*   *   *

I hear often that because the police associations are in favour of the registry, it must be a good thing. I appreciate that policing is a tough, risky profession with many knowledgeable people in the force. However, the police are no more infallible than are our judges, doctors, or other authorities. Informed criticism is a fundamental requirement in a democracy. I hope the following detail is considered constructively in light of all its ramifications and the reasons for which I offer it.

Although police associations officially support the registry, there is much dissention in the ranks. For example, Constable John Gayder wrote a very thoughtful article that was given me by a policeman. This article was posted on an Internet site devoted to the gun registry debate. In this article, he commented, "The system will prove to be as disastrously misguided as leech therapy, shock treatment and Thalidomide were to the field of medicine."

The police chiefs to whom I spoke admitted that if the inaccuracies and costs I predicted did occur, then the usefulness of the system would be limited. This type of situation is not uncommon. I witnessed it many times in business and elsewhere in the computer environment. So many people observe the fantastic role the computer has played in the space program and elsewhere and assume the computer is all but foolproof and therefore don't apply due diligence in scrutinizing proposals.

Police Chief V. J. MacDonald, who was president of the Association of Chiefs of Police at the time of the registry proposal, wrote a position paper that was circulated by the association and printed in the *Globe and Mail* in 1995. In this paper, he stated that a condition for police support was that "the federal government has promised that the cost will not be downloaded on police and that fees will be nominal to promote compliance." Are we all not inclined to be less critical of a freebie? It is a reason promoters give away tickets to events. A consultant who did work for the police force stated that one of the reasons police chiefs supported the system was that they viewed it as a way to bootstrap the rank and file into the computer age at someone else's expense. Mr. Rock emphasized many times that the registry would not be an expense to the police, that they would receive additional funding for their role in its operation, and that it would not divert any officers from street patrol.

Let's not overlook the fact that politicians allot the money for police budgets and have an influence in the appointment and salary of police chiefs. In all walks of life, such power is usually a factor in what recipients think, say, and do. Also, the chiefs in any organization have a position of authority that influences what subordinates say and do. A father of a police officer pointed the foregoing out to me and said it was the reason his son, who was hoping for a promotion, was staying silent about his concerns.

A year into the implementation, the RCMP expressed concern about inaccuracies, critical resource shortages, and soaring costs. At that time, less than 2 percent of all shotguns and rifles had been registered, and the old handgun registry was still in operation. Police officers were being assigned registry duties despite the promise that no frontline officers would be diverted from street patrol. Ontario's attorney general wrote that the costs being incurred would support an additional 1,900 frontline officers, which he felt would be far more effective in fighting crime. The police association asked for an audit and threatened to withdraw support.

Let me now turn to my observations to the political party in power and the justice minister, Mr. Rock, who pushed this project through. Perhaps what follows may be too harsh on the man. Maybe he was doing what his boss, the prime minister, told him to do. I think I detected this as he became more aware of the firearms situation. I also observed that he is an intelligent man with much energy and many leadership qualities. Perhaps these qualities were not effectively harnessed. Perhaps his experience has made him wiser so that he will be a valuable asset to our country and the world in the long run.

Allan Rock said, "I came to Ottawa with the firm belief that the only people in this country who should have guns are police officers and soldiers." Although he later seemed to discover that there are other people in this vast country who have valid reasons for possession of firearms—aboriginals, trappers, farmers, hunters, and sports shooters—we know that underlying beliefs tend to be a factor in thinking. This certainly appears to be the case in the development of the firearms registry and its administration procedures.

The ruling party's methods displayed a political posturing culture that a growing number of political pundits criticize. The culture is overly self-centred, more interested in power than providing the investigative skills and the leadership we expect and need from elected representatives. Too often, polls are relied on as a basis for policy development and justification rather than applied as indicators.

Mr. Rock and other politicians also displayed traits that I find unsupportable, traits which many people brush aside as "politics." The amount of crime involving guns was emphasized to a level that many suggest was fearmongering. Policemen who expressed concerns about making criminals out of normally law-abiding people were told that, of course, police would be allowed to use their discretion on any perceived breaches of strict rules built into the registry. When the same concerns were expressed by aboriginals and trappers, the answer was that there would be no exceptions. At one point, Mr. Rock said that if implementation of the system costs more than $85 million, it would be cancelled. He later revised his estimate to $120 million. When actual costs were approaching $1 billion, he was asked if he was withdrawing his support for the registry. He pointed out that he was no longer involved, had a new assignment, and discredited the figures.

I detected a self-centred approach often used by many ambitious individuals in business and elsewhere. This is the formula—identify a problem, exaggerate it, offer a solution, discredit opposition, get promoted to implement, get moved to another position before the inadequacies become apparent, and blame successors for overruns.

To justify implementation of the registry, the government quoted polls that showed a majority favoured gun registration of all firearms. Part of the reason for this is the way the question was worded. Other polls were ignored that showed the majority were unaware of cost of the system, existing gun controls, and their implications. For example, most people were unaware that all handguns had required registration since the 1930s. Hundreds of weapons are classified as restricted or banned, but these still frequently show up in the hands of criminals.

At the proposal stage of the new registry system, I felt it worthwhile to share my knowledge and perspectives with Mr. Rock who was my member of Parliament. I had voted for him. I wrote a fairly detailed commentary and asked for a meeting with him and two recently retired police officers that I knew. He replied with a three-page form letter that reiterated all the points he made in his public meetings and speeches, the very points I was addressing as flawed. I called his campaign manager whom I knew well and asked if he would meet with me to discuss the subject. He wouldn't nor would he read what I had written and lectured me a bit on the inappropriateness of criticizing the registry system because I was, after all, a card-carrying liberal.

I then talked to the consultant who attended the government's information meetings as an expert. I discovered that she had an excellent formal education and good computer knowledge in some areas. She shared with me the new technology in the system she was proposing. I knew such a system was great for many applications but would not meet either the functional requirements stated or goals, due to the scattered environment of firearms, needed for rapid response time to inquiries and problems of serial number identification. She wasn't prepared to hear what I had to say. This added to my concerns. (Unless you are a gun collector, you probably won't understand problems with serial numbers on guns. An RCMP expert stated he would have little confidence in a registration number of a rifle unless he saw the gun and registered it himself. He was also concerned about duplications.)

To reconfirm that I was on the right track, I talked to three more knowledgeable computer people with expertise in areas that had unique inventory requirements similar to those of the firearms registry. They agreed with me. I discussed the issue with several more policemen and read some pertinent reports that they suggested. Confident in my assessment, I decided to try an approach that sometimes sways a politician—signatures of voters on a petition. So I started canvassing. Most of the people I canvassed are relatively successful, professional people, so I was a bit surprised to find that over 70 percent were in favour of the gun registry but had scant knowledge on the subject. I then supplied them with information about existing laws, the type of system that would be needed, its cost, and evidence that it would not be effective. A total of 90 percent then signed the petition against the registry. The 10 percent who was still in favour thought there should be no guns and were not open to a discussion on the issue.

Gary Mauser did a more in-depth study than me but with similar observations. Many who still want the system seem to view it as a security blanket.

As the reality of the system becomes more obvious, there are growing numbers of people who feel it is regrettable that billions of dollars have been, and are continuing to be, siphoned away from effective police resources and other worthy activities.

In the article "How the Liberals Shot the Truth" published in December 2002 in the *Globe and Mail*, Margaret Wente explained that when she asked Philip Stenning, a leading expert on firearms policy and a professor with the University of Toronto's Centre of Criminology, how we got into the billion-dollar mess, he answered, "Ideology and incompetence."

The registry system and its policies is a prime example that illustrates the claim of pundits that the government's ability to do good is equal to its ability to do harm. One more reason, I suggest, that the actions of governments require close scrutiny.

I am certain that there are better approaches than some of our current attempts at crime reduction.

CHAPTER 15

More points to ponder

The following sent to me by e-mail makes an interesting point.

Marine Corp's General Reinwald was interviewed on the radio the other day and you have to read his reply to the lady who interviewed him concerning guns and children. Regardless of how you feel about gun laws you gotta love this! It is a portion of National Public Radio (NPR) interview between a female broadcaster and US Marine Corps General Reinwald who was about to sponsor a Boy Scout Troop visiting his military installation.

FEMALE INTERVIEWER:
So, General Reinwald, what things are you going to teach these young boys when they visit your base?

GENERAL REINWALD:
We're going to teach them climbing, canoeing, archery, and shooting.

FEMALE INTERVIEWER:
Shooting! That's a bit irresponsible, isn't it?

GENERAL REINWALD:
I don't see why, they'll be properly supervised on the rifle range.

FEMALE INTERVIEWER:
Don't you admit that this is a terribly dangerous activity to be teaching children?

GENERAL REINWALD:
I don't see how. We will be teaching them proper rifle discipline before they even touch a firearm.

FEMALE INTERVIEWER:
But you're equipping them to become violent killers.

GENERAL REINWALD:
Well, Ma'am, you're equipped to be a prostitute, but you're not one, are you?

The interview ended.

Perhaps more attention needs to be given to the adage:

> *Good people do not need laws to tell them to act responsibly, while bad people will find ways around the laws.*
> —Plato, 347 BC

The Internet is exposing us to many things that people can misuse, and this further complicates the development of suitable laws that can be enforced. This is frustrating, and I think will force society to look for alternate ways to deal with misuse of products.

*　　*　　*

Several acquaintances suggested that I should see Michael Moore's *Bowling for Columbine*. The opening scene shows people shooting at targets that flip over when hit and then pop back up like bowling pins. The inference made by my acquaintances is that this type of activity was a contributing factor to the terrible atrocity at Columbine where twelve students and a teacher were shot and killed and twenty-three injured by two fellow students. I pointed out my interpretation of this scene as being entirely different from theirs. Targets, for instance, are used to train policemen, including our highly respected mounted police and others. This does not turn them into criminals. In fact, all shooting ranges have similar facilities, and the training people there build safety consciousness and responsibility. After I thought about other scenes and the overall meaning, it appears to me that the thrust of the movie is really about a nation of fear that is jumping in every direction to find fault and not getting to the heart of the problem. Similar to the frightened squirrel, they are doing things that are actually harmful in the long run.

A beneficial result of shooting at targets was verified for me recently at a pellet gun-shooting contest at a Toronto hotel. Participants came from dozens of countries around the world. There were categories for teenage girls and boys, adults, and the disadvantaged. Their shooting skills at retrievable targets were awesome, and their enthusiasm and behaviour inspiring. Off the range, they proudly showed one another their guns and talked about ballistics and craftsmanship in their tools. The event was first class, similar to the Olympics. It was, in fact, a qualifying round for the Olympics.

Nonetheless, when a youth with a pellet gun recently shot another boy in Toronto, there was a hue and a cry to have pellet guns banned or restricted in a way that would seriously hinder participation in competitions such as described above. The irony is that the restrictions will never prevent reckless youths from making a slingshot, blowgun, or grenade or from taking a car and using it irresponsibly. One wonders where the parents were when the youth obtained the pellet gun and what counselling and supervision they provided on proper use. I realize that even good, careful parents can't always teach a child not to do silly things, and you can't blame parents for the impulsive acts of kids. But neither can the importance of good parenting and mentoring be overlooked.

I find it regrettable that valuable youth training programs on conservation and associated outdoor activities are so often rejected by schools and parents when such programs are offered by organizations that explain hunting as an element in conservation—an approach that entails safety training in the use of firearms.

*   *   *

There should be little doubt that the fear of firearms is causing society to do unproductive things. It is generally agreed by those knowledgeable in human behaviour that most of us don't recognize this fear. There is much evidence that it is causing wasted energy in unproductive actions and health problems.

Darrell Scott, the father of Rachel Scott, a victim of the Columbine High School shootings in Littleton, Colorado, was invited to address the House Judiciary Committee's subcommittee. What he said to the national leaders during this special session of Congress was painfully truthful and not what they wanted to hear.

The following is a portion of the transcript:

Since the dawn of creation there has been both good and evil in the hearts of men and women. We all contain the seeds of kindness or the seeds of violence.

The death of my wonderful daughter, Rachel Joy Scott, and the deaths of that heroic teacher, and the other twelve children who died must not be in vain. Their blood cries out for answers. The first recorded act of violence was when Cain slew his brother Abel out in the field. The villain was not the club he used. Neither was it the NCA, the National Club Association. The true killer was Cain, and the reason for the murder could only be found in Cain's heart.

In the days that followed the Columbine tragedy, I was amazed at how quickly fingers began to be pointed at groups such as the NRA. I am not a member of the NRA. I am not a hunter. I do not even own a gun. I am not here to represent or defend the NRA—because I don't believe that they are responsible for my daughter's death. Therefore I do not believe that they need to be defended. If I believed they had anything to do with Rachel's murder I would be their strongest opponent.

I am here today to declare that Columbine was not just a tragedy—it was a spiritual event that should be forcing us to look at where the real blame lies! Much of the blame lies here in this room. Much of the blame lies behind the pointing fingers of the accusers themselves. I wrote a poem that expresses my feelings best. This was written way before I knew I would be speaking here today:

Your laws ignore our deepest needs, your words are empty air.
You've stripped away our heritage; You've outlawed simple prayer.
Now gunshots fill our classrooms, and precious children die.
You seek for answers everywhere, and ask the question "Why?"
You regulate restrictive laws, through legislative creed.
And yet you fail to understand, That God is what we need!

Men and women are three-part beings. We all consist of body, soul, and spirit. When we refuse to acknowledge a third part of our make-up, we create a void that allows evil, prejudice, and hatred to rush in and reek havoc. Spiritual influences were present within our educational systems for most of our nation's history. Many of our major colleges began as theological seminaries. This is a historical fact. What has happened to us as a nation?

We have refused to honour God, and in so doing, we open the doors to hatred and violence. And when something as terrible as Columbine's tragedy occurs, politicians immediately look for a scapegoat such as the NRA. They immediately seek to pass more restrictive laws that contribute to erode away our personal and private liberties. We do not need more restrictive laws.

No number of gun laws can stop someone who spends months planning this type of massacre. The real villain lies within our own hearts. Political posturing and restrictive legislation are not the answers.

CHAPTER 16

Life is a paradox

Almost every wise saying has an opposite one,
no less wise, to balance it.
—George Santayana

The test of a first-rate intelligence is the ability to hold two
opposite ideas in the mind at the same time and still retain
the ability to function. One should, for example, be able to see
that things are hopeless and yet be determined to make them
otherwise.

—F. Scott Fitzgerald

The winds and the waves are always on the
side of the ablest navigators.
—Edward Gibbon

One outcome that grew from my deliberations is that I view life as even more of a paradox and find my ability to recognize, reconcile, and balance dualities a valuable asset for coping with many situations in life, including the dilemmas in hunting. In chapter 2, "A Mysterious Message and Ensuing Information," I stated that I would further explore paradoxes in this chapter.

Paradoxes are sometimes referred to as the duality of life. Certainly, we are constantly faced with dilemmas. They appear to be fundamental component in the nature of things.

Recognizing the world of dualities can make a huge difference in our capacity to improve results. Many peak-performance coaches say it empowers a person to achieve a higher state of consciousness and fulfillment.

Pondering paradoxes can be both interesting and illuminating:

> Through adversity comes strength.
> A person's weakness is his strength.
> There are two sides to every story.

Richard Tarnas in his best seller, *The Passion of the Western Mind: Understanding the Ideas that Have Shaped Our World View*, makes reference to numerous paradoxes that have perplexed great thinkers and scientists throughout the ages. Examples: The world around us bears signs of both order and chaos. For every action, there is an equal and opposite reaction.

Niels Bohr's axiom in quantum physics is, "The opposite of a profound truth may well be another truth."

Tarnas's explanation of the following paradox takes up many pages in his book. He suggests that understanding the nature of paradoxes has tremendous significance in this rapidly changing technological world in which we are flooded with new findings and theories. Some are important, others perhaps can be discarded, while still others need to be challenged because they are misleading or false. He points out that man comes into this world with some innate knowledge on which he builds through experiences and teachings. Man needs some basic information and standards to successfully cope with life. Being sceptical of ideas that are different or new is a wise and necessary trait. We can't, nor should we, start each day with a "blank sheet of paper" or accept every passing popular idea.

There is no doubt that humans are predisposed to adopting the predominate ideas of the times. Information repeated often enough has a way of infiltrating the mind as true, especially if supported by leaders or authorities and are eloquently presented. Once an idea infiltrates the mind, individuals naturally tend to resist other ideas that challenge their perception and frequently overlook evidence that supports a different point of view. We tend to carry our perceptions, both the helpful and harmful, from one generation to the next as well as from one relationship to the next.

Holding too firmly to our perceptions has detrimental effects. It can limit or close off inquiry to the point where one can be misled or not be open to new evidence, new discoveries, and valuable points of view. A few outstanding examples: the arguments against the concept of a spinning Earth and the persecution of persons with such heretical notions. Similarly, there were those who dogmatically claimed Earth revolved around the sun as well as those who claimed the world was flat. For how many centuries did the belief in the "divine right of kings" linger?

Dr. Jesse Roche, the eminent researcher who in 1980 found insulin not just in the human brain but also in one-cell creatures outside the human body, was ridiculed for several years by the reigning medical belief. Everyone "knew" that the pancreas was needed to make insulin.

I find this state of affairs to be quite common and is certainly evident in the hunting debate.

> *Be fruitful and multiply, and replenish the earth, and subdue it: and have domination over the fish of the sea, and over the fowl of the air, and over every living thing that moveth upon the earth.*
> —God to Adam, Genesis 1:28

> *Thou shalt not kill.*
> —God to Moses, Exodus 20:13

> *You will know you have found God when you will not murder (that is willfully kill without cause). For while you will understand that you cannot end another's life (all life is eternal) you will not choose to terminate any particular carnation, nor change any life form to another, without the most sacred justification. Your new reverence for life will cause you to honour all life forms—including plants, trees, and animals—and to impact them only when it is for the highest good . . . These are your freedoms, not your restrictions.*
> —God in Neale Walsch's book *Conversations with God*

> *All life lives by killing and eating lives. The reconciliation of mind to this condition of life is fundamental to all creation stories.*
> —Joseph Campbell, American preeminent scholar and teacher

Mark Twain tackled a paradox with which he struggled as only he could. Twain had been raised in a religious environment where overcoming sexual desires was considered a saintly quality that improved one's chances of getting to heaven. As a result, he struggled with debilitating guilt over his sexuality and wondered if a toad, which has sex only once a year, had a better chance of getting to heaven than he did.

Loving oneself is a wonderful quality. Without it, we would be unable to love others; yet excessive self-love is narcissism, which is a deterrent to healthy relationships.

Denis Waitley, American author and peak-performance expert, poses this enigma, "You must stick to your conviction, but be ready to abandon your assumptions."

To me, these words of wisdom by Waitley illustrate an interesting paradox:

> *Loving people live in a loving world.*
> *Hostile people live in a hostile world.*
> *Same world.*

Kris Kristofferson, musician and songwriter, sought happiness and freedom through alcohol, drugs, and divorce. They didn't deliver what he was seeking. He wrote in his hit ballad "Me and Bobby Mcgee," "Freedom is just another word for 'nothing left to lose'"—another paradox.

This paradox came to light recently. DDT, which was hailed as a wonderful substance to control unwanted insects, was used extensively outdoors for many years by farmers and others. When harmful effects were observed on birds, small animals, and indicated in humans in North America, DDT was essentially banned. Now a very strong case is being presented supporting proper use of DDT as a good thing, especially in countries where malaria is a major health hazard. In Africa, it is estimated that over one thousand children die daily of malaria and that proper use of DDT indoors would prevent 90 percent of these deaths.

The use of many prescription drugs is a paradox that needs better recognition and management. A proper balance between good and bad effects is crucial.

Many of man's tools can be used for good or bad. Firearms are the perfect example. They have many valuable applications—defence and security, helping in the process of supplying food, pest and animal control and conservation, ending the life of suffering animals, sports shooting and hunting to name a few. And then they can be misused and too often are.

John F. Kennedy, thirty-fifth American president, said, "If a free society cannot help the many who are poor, it cannot save the few who are rich." Another well-known similar idea is, "From each according to his ability, to each according to his need." Most of us probably agree that there is much merit in these statements. But any concept carried too far or legislated can produce negative results, most vividly illustrated in the doctrines of many communist countries as well as in some of our own social programs.

Frequently, dilemmas and possible outcomes related to them are just not recognized. Kindness is a good example—kindly parents sometimes give their children everything they want with the intention of making them happy but without consideration that this conditioning can cause unhappiness later in life when the child does not receive everything he or she expects. Such children have not been prepared for the harsh realities of life. There are valid reasons for the old expression "killing with kindness." Dr. Phil refers to this form of "kindness" as the worst form of child abuse.

Nonetheless, some people don't accept the dilemma of opposites for various reasons. Some people claim paradoxes only exist when there is a flaw in the individual—such as unclear thinking or an inability to be in touch with the authentic self or a lack of holiness or love. Some mystics claim there are mystical experiences that help dissolve the alienation of duality but don't eliminate them. Maybe there are some who don't experience dilemmas; but for most of us, paradoxes emerge as a result of the cards dealt to us by nature though you may prefer another identification such as God, Allah, or the Great Spirit.

Ralph Waldo Emerson said, "Every vice is only an exaggeration of a necessary and virtuous function." Isn't this a paradox?

There is no doubt that hunting is a paradox. Proper participation reaps many benefits. Improper participation is harmful.

EPILOGUE

When I began putting pen to paper, my intent was to explain the importance of our hunting heritage. I wanted to nurture an understanding of hunting for those who choose not to hunt. For those who do, I hoped to encourage responsibility among hunters and help us all towards a more common ground. The story developed to encompass more—all of which, I believe, enhances my original purpose while offering other worthwhile observations.

Many wise people throughout the ages have promoted the idea that animals offer us guidance, wisdom, and support if we are open to it. But many of us are dubious about such ideas. On the other hand, maybe some of our senses that could help us have been allowed to atrophy through modern living. I mentioned in the introduction that the catalyst for this book was an experience with a large bull moose and thoughts about it offered by a psychic. One of the things the psychic said was, "The reason he (the moose) jumped up in front of Ralph was to raise his awareness. He wants Ralph to explain to others that hunting is part of nature."

I was my somewhat sceptical self about the entire conversation and did not attach significance to the phrase "raise his awareness." However, in the process of writing, I have explored my understanding of the nature of various aspects in life, perhaps more fully than ever before. My "awareness" has, in fact, been raised albeit in a roundabout way. I have developed a renewed reverence for the magical ways in which Mother Nature works and the importance of taking personal responsibility for our own lives. I have become more conscious of the intrinsic ways that animals have learned altruistic behaviours of sharing, conservation of food supply, and other survival lessons that compliment "survival of the fittest." I have become more discerning about my perceptions, the aliveness of all matter, the many weaknesses of our democratic system, and some of the strange and sometimes surprising ways that help our wits grow sharper.

For me, life remains a mysterious and wonderful journey. I look in a similar way upon the events brought about by my encounter with my spirit moose. For reasons that I don't fully understand, I was sparked to write this document.

*   *   *

I have often thought that studies done with offspring of chimps have profound implications for our species and life on this planet. The scientists behind this research knew what was needed to raise a healthy baby chimp by a real mother, so they created a "wire mother"—a lifelike mannequin. The nipples, attached to a special baby bottle, supplied all the nutrients a chimp is known to need—the same that would come from its real mother's milk. Despite the fact that the baby chimp could climb up on their wired mother for warmth, safety, and the same nutrition, the chimps with the wire mothers withered and died.

It appears to me that as we live more and more in an environment of growing concrete, steel, pavement, television, and electronic gadgetry, we too are opting for a "wire Mother Earth" and spending less and less time experiencing and bonding with nature. Without connection to the real Mother Earth, our roots, and heritage, we are also withering, leaving us susceptible to inner turmoil and further susceptibility to the various social problems. Hunting can help provide a connection to Mother Earth, one that strengthens individuals and alleviates many of these problems.

There are, however, powerful lobbies allied and intent on discouraging hunting, and in our form of democracy, there is an inclination for elected representatives to establish rules and laws to pacify those who have developed influential political clout and claim the support of opinion polls. They are motivated to do this to gain votes and thus keep their jobs. Unfortunately, many popular ideas as expressed through such polls are too often based on insufficient or misleading information. It takes hard work to research the complexities in any issue, to sort the wheat from the chaff, and to develop appropriate policy. It then takes special leadership skills to create bridges of understanding across this vast, diverse country. Inappropriate decisions are often the result of not doing the needed homework.

I point out previously in this document that hunting organizations spend millions of dollars presenting their case to the politicians. However, too often, the politicians make their decisions based on polls where the majority are nonhunters. The cancellation of the spring bear hunt is but one example.

Too many people in democracies put a misplaced faith in political leaders and political parties. Too often, we simply trust our politicians to do what is right and do little to participate in governance or share the specific knowledge we have. Democracy, we need no reminding, is not a spectator sport.

I have tried to show that government policies often backfire. Time and again, a seemingly nifty policy is ineffective or produces the opposite of what was intended. Our politicians' flawed methods can lead us down paths that not only hurt hunting but attack its economic, social, and spiritual benefits as well. The methods used too often result in waste in other areas as well. Another concern of mine is the use, too often, of emotional tactics that incite an exaggerated fear. Watch closely for the demonizing of people with opposing views on the subject of firearms.

Exaggerating fear often garners votes for the perpetrator but is not conducive to rational thinking and decision making. The examples I have given are illustrations only. They are the tip of an iceberg, a wake-up call for us to take a closer look at our own perceptions and how our country is governed.

* * *

Our Charter of Human Rights and Freedoms designed to protect minorities is not effective in many cases. Hunters are a minority, and I caution all hunters not to rely on the Charter to protect their rights to hunt. There is concern that not even judges are immune to bias and the pressures of the majority. The chief justice of Ontario, Roy McMurtry, in a recent address to senior provincial and federal judges stressed, "Judges must continue to uphold the rights of minorities—even if it means overturning the will of the majority. I believe that when the majority takes away the rights of a minority, that is not democracy. Democracy is, therefore, a delicate balance between majority rule and individual rights."

* * *

I have a real concern about having to justify hunting. If society demands to know people's needs for their personal choices and then judges such needs by the tastes, standards, or morals of others, it opens the door to oppression and intolerance. If we must establish need as a justification, we may not be entitled to much beyond basic food and shelter. Others who feel differently about our habits and tastes may pass laws to ban just about anything.

There is, in man's nature, a tendency to form opinions based on scant evidence. This characteristic has a good side. There is always the danger that we could spend so much time investigating that little else would get accomplished. On the negative side, however, too little research can lead to unsound opinions that lead to flawed results. Too often, opinions seem to be based on emotion rather than rational thinking. In fact, many of our opinions originate from our parents and our experiences prior to the age of six or seven. I suggest that opinions too often take the form of judgements. Judgements are my primary concern in this document because by judging, we frequently attempt to impose our way of thinking on others. A frequent recommendation made by therapists/psychologists/psychiatrists is, "Don't be so judgemental."

It is our judgements, after all, more so than our differences that cause us problems.

It is one thing to choose not to do something. Imposing restrictions on others based on our beliefs and opinions, on the other hand, is a reflection of the darker side of human nature.

Benjamin Franklin cautioned in 1759, "Those that give up essential liberty to obtain a little temporary safety deserve neither liberty nor safety."

Let's not overlook Louis D. Brandeis, supreme court judge and highly regarded thinker, who warned, "The greatest dangers to liberty lurk in insidious encroachment by men of zeal, well-meaning, but without understanding."

Perhaps we would be better served by rethinking who and what we are, what we are afraid of, and what is actually harmful. Maybe, then, a more accurate diagnosis of the real problems would be forthcoming. This, in my opinion, is essential before effective solutions can be prescribed.

*   *   *

One of the comments I frequently hear is that there is no longer any opportunity to hunt within a reasonable distance of Toronto where I live. Actually, because of the great successes with the introduction of wild turkey by hunters in Southern Ontario and the tremendous increase of deer, there is an abundance of opportunity within an hour or two of the city. Many farmers, if approached properly, welcome responsible hunters to reduce the number of wild animals that are eating or destroying their crops, gardens, and trees. Similar situations are developing in many regions across North America.

*   *   *

In the debate about hunting, one question that needs answering is, who is being harmed by legitimate hunters? Training has made it one of our safest sports. Not a single wildlife species that is hunted in Ontario is declining because of hunting. This is true across this land.

*   *   *

I hope I have been able to make a case that supports responsible hunting and wilderness experience and that we continue on a proper course with our wildlife-management concepts.

> *Hunting is so important to so many people still today. Up to 75 percent of hunters are reportedly motivated to hunt each year because hunting connects them psychologically to nature like no other activity.*
> —a statement from the North America Wildlife and Natural Resources Conference, 2001

A major education campaign is required to change attitudes about hunting. In our urban population centres especially, the majority is not in favour of hunting, and many are vocally and loudly against it. Because they make up about 80 percent of voters, they are a primary influence on our political leaders.

There is no doubt that humans are predisposed to adopting the predominate ideas of the times. It is this feature on which propaganda and advertising thrives. Information repeated often enough has a way of infiltrating the mind as true, especially if supported by leaders or authorities and are eloquently presented. Once an idea infiltrates the mind, individuals naturally tend to resist other ideas that challenge their perception, and they frequently overlook, often subconsciously, any evidence that supports a different point of view. I am sympathetic to this condition, building on our experiences and previous knowledge, and being sceptical of ideas that are different or new is a wise and necessary trait that enables humans to function effectively. We can't, nor should we, start each day with a "blank sheet of paper" or accept every passing popular idea. On the other hand, holding too firmly to our perceptions has detrimental effects. It can limit or close off inquiry to the point where one can be misled or not open to new evidence, new discoveries, and valuable points of view.

In terms of improved health, happiness, and crime reduction, a growing number of researchers are advocating the benefits of wilderness experience; and the more it approximates the hunter-gatherer model, the greater the benefit.

The rewards as a path to personal improvement and the betterment of society may not be statistically provable as yet. However, an easily observable truism is that one cannot be thankful and depressed or unhappy at the same time. That unhappiness is a stressful condition that contributes to absences from work, headaches, and other health problems is also true. Exposure to the hardships of a wilderness experience makes us more thankful, normally, for the comforts we have.

There are signs of young spirits wanting to reconnect to Mother Earth and her animals through hunting and back-to-nature experiences. The success of the Get Outdoors youth program sponsored by the Ontario Federation of Anglers and Hunters is an example. A search on the Internet for youth wilderness and hunting training lists hundreds of programs.

We are fortunate in Canada to have such vast areas suitable for wildlife and for wilderness experiences. I believe these resources are sustainable if everyone contributes to the conditions needed to achieve this goal. But we will need to give greater heed to the fact that our urban lifestyle is hurting the environment. Too many people live as if their actions have no bearing on the natural world—as if they are totally separate from it. Hunters know better. They know we are all part of nature. Let's take a closer look at the growing evidence that wilderness exposure can bring about many improvements including happiness, less reliance on expensive medications, less drug addiction, and less crime.

Some of the reasons for these positive effects remain a mystery. Scientist and researcher Dr. Candace B. Pert has provided evidence of the biochemistry basis for the mind-body connection that has been proclaimed by sages for centuries. She says, "I have come to believe that virtually all illness, if not psychosomatic in foundation, has a definite psychosomatic component." She points out that the molecules of our emotions are inseparable from physiology—it is the emotions that link mind and body.

Emotions affect how we do research as well as how we stay healthy or become ill. She states emphatically that we must take responsibility for the way we feel. Consciously or unconsciously, we are choosing how we feel at every single moment; and these feelings affect every aspect of our physiology, producing blissful good health or miserable disease. She strongly advocates getting in touch with our natural self—spending time in nature, meditation, relaxation, and exercise—and the avoidance of drugs (both legal and illegal). The aim is emotional wholeness—to live in a reverent state and to trust your body and mind to heal and improve itself. Also, she advises, we should erase all thoughts that do not promote happiness and wellness such as hurts, anger, and fear.

Hunters would be wise to become more knowledgeable in all of this and do much more as mentors and facilitators to create a greater insight into the significance of hunting, thus ensuring continuing availability of the resource. A tad more empathy might help too. The self-righteous attitude of some hunters does nothing to endear them to opponents.

Our privilege to hunt and use firearms has to be supported with valid reasoning and rational explanation. Implying we have a right to hunt will never convince others of the merits of hunting.

Too many hunters say there is nothing they can do to change the minds of those who don't support hunting. This attitude is allowing the antihunting groups to squeeze the life out of a valuable pursuit.

* * *

Imagine what could be accomplished if some of the huge resources spent on the military for protection (worldwide over $1 trillion; Canada in 2005, $20 billion) were redirected to help Mother Nature protect and sustain our natural resources. In addition, consider this: Canada spent $141 billion on health care and $15 billion on justice in 2005—$5,200 for every Canadian. Is it possible that expenditures could be reduced by applying methods examined in this document? I think so. These savings could then be redirected to helping Mother Nature achieve further benefits, a bit like a snowball effect. As radical as this may appear, we should remind ourselves that if there is the will, there is a way.

Perhaps it's time for radical new thinking. Spending for health care is escalating at an unsustainable rate according to most experts on the subject. Illness is increasing—there are six times as many doctors per capita than when I was a boy. There is also about four times the number of policemen per capita. Studies indicate that 40 percent of cancers are caused by anger/fear. Many experts say that stress, fear, and anger, which have their roots in unrealistic expectations, actually cause 80 to 90 percent of all illness. These same emotions are the primary source of violence and crime.

*   *   *

*If you talk to the animals they will talk with you and you will
    know each other.
If you do not talk to them you will not know them, and what you
    do not know you will fear.
What one fears one destroys.*

—Chief Dan George